SEEING
THE WHOLE
THROUGH
SOCIAL STUDIES

SEEING
THE WHOLE
THROUGH
SOCIAL STUDIES

Tarry Lindquist

HEINEMANN
PORTSMOUTH, NH

Heinemann
A division of Reed Elsevier Inc.
361 Hanover Street
Portsmouth, NH 03801-3912

Offices and agents throughout the world

Acknowledgments for previously published material begin on page 203.

Library of Congress Cataloging-in-Publication Data

Lindquist, Tarry.
    Seeing the whole through social studies / by Tarry Lindquist.
      p. cm.
    Includes bibliographical references.
    ISBN 0-435-08902-1 (acid-free paper)
     1. Social sciences—Study and teaching.   I. Title.
    H62.L4844   1995
    300—dc20   94-48190
                                                           CIP

Editor: Carolyn Coman
Production: Renée M. Pinard
Interior and Cover Design: Joni Doherty
Interior Photographs: Judith Slepyan

Printed in the United States of America on acid-free paper.
99 98 97 96 95 EB 1 2 3 4 5

To Malcolm, Tia, and Tani
This trip wasn't alone either!
Love you!

THE MOUSE MORAL

KNOWING IN PART MAY MAKE A FINE TALE,
BUT WISDOM COMES FROM SEEING THE WHOLE.

Ed Young, *Seven Blind Mice*

CONTENTS

FOREWORD

When Emily Dickinson wrote, "I dwell in possibilities . . . not wishing to miss the dawn, I open every door," she could have been describing Tarry Lindquist. Tarry dwells in possibilities, and her book opens an intimate door into her classroom. Tarry is a teacher's teacher who communicates her love of children and enthusiasm for teaching on each page of this book.

You will travel through the school year as Tarry shares the journey she has taken to reconstruct her teaching day and to develop an integrated curriculum. As you read this book, you will feel as though you are watching the day unfold in Tarry's classroom—a classroom where good things happen for children. The story of Tarry's classroom is one of valuing each child, respecting ideas, and being concerned for the common good. Tarry shares her insights in practical terms, thus providing a helpful model for others.

Tarry begins with the children in her classroom and their needs. She weaves their needs and aspirations into a rich tapestry of teaching and learning experiences. Classroom ideas for integrating the curriculum abound, but this is much more than a book of teaching ideas. Tarry offers a structure and purpose for integrating the curriculum. In this book, curriculum decisions are grounded in sound learning theory and best practice.

For the teacher just beginning the process of integrating the curriculum, this book is a must. It provides inspiration and a realistic assessment of what's possible on the journey toward holistic learning experiences. If you are a teacher already in the midst of integrating the curriculum, you'll find a soulmate who shares freely her successes and her challenges.

Seeing the Whole is a story of one teacher who has opened the door to a multitude of possibilities. Walking with Tarry through that door on the journey to holistic learning is an inspiration.

> Margit McGuire, Professor and Chair, Teacher Education
> Seattle University
> Past President, National Council for the Social Studies

ACKNOWLEDGMENTS

Where to begin, that's the question.

I wish to acknowledge the support and love I've had from my dad and honor the memory of my mother.

Special thanks to the Class of 2001, their parents, and the wonderful people I work with every day at Lakeridge Elementary.

Thanks to all the kids who've taken the time to teach me and to those kids who have given me permission to share their products and pictures. Thanks to their parents for trusting me to teach their kids.

Thanks to my principal, John Cameron, and school secretary, Peggy Chapman, for providing support and friendship. Thanks to the Lakeridge lunch bunch, who offer so much wisdom and laughter. Thanks to Nancy Kezner and Carole Muth, both of whom laugh and cry with me as we live, learn, and teach. Thanks to Paula Fraser, who responded to the draft with an intuitive and intellectual eye, to Barbara Inman, who added wisdom, to Jan Allman, who asked key questions, and Katie Roberts McLean, who inspired me to become a teacher.

Some people have profoundly affected my teaching and me. Over the years, they have invited me to learn at their institutions, sharing of themselves and helping me grow as a person and as a teacher. Those people include Gary Howard of the Respecting Ethnic and Cultural Heritage (REACH) Center, Mary Bernson of the East Asia Resource Center, Alita Letwin of the Center for Civic Education, Julie Van Camp from the Center for Research and Development for Law-Related Education (CRADLE), Margaret Armancas-Fisher and Julia Gold of University of Puget Sound Citizen Education in the Law, Harvey Segal of the Community College of Micronesia, Ann Sweeney from the Office for the Administrator of the Courts, Jane Brem and Margit McGuire of Seattle University, Gary Phillips from the School Improvement Project, Larry Strickland of the Washington State Office of the Superintendent of Public Instruction, and Frank Koontz of the Bureau of Education and Research.

Thanks to my colleagues on the National Council for the Social Studies Board of Directors, the Advanced Certification for Teachers of Social Studies Committee, and the Middle Childhood/Generalist Committee of the National Board for Professional Teaching Standards, who have helped me verbalize what I believe about teaching and learning and who have encouraged me to continue my quest for an integrated, holistic curriculum.

Thanks to Judi Slepyan, who tirelessly gives of her time and talent to photograph the children of Lakeridge exploring, learning, and caring. I am so pleased to share her photos, the result of a very special combination of head, hands, and heart.

Thanks to my husband's family, especially the eighteen who are teachers.

Heartfelt thanks to Marte Peet, Oralee Kramer, and Rick Moulden, who read and reread this manuscript, listened to me talk it through, and still said they wanted a copy.

Thanks to Carolyn Coman, who was willing to give me a chance to publish a book that wasn't stapled, would stand up on a shelf, and would have an ISBN. Thanks to Alan Huisman, who edited the manuscript.

Finally, warm thanks to my husband, Malcolm, a true partner in this book, creating graphics, conquering computer questions, and constantly providing support in a dozen different ways. Malcolm, and our two daughters, Tia and Tani, kept telling me I could write a book and then made it possible for me to try.

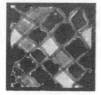

INTRODUCTION
Reflections from a Classroom Teacher

I teach. And in my heart of hearts, every time I teach social studies, I believe that maybe, just maybe, this lesson is the one that will provide the skills, knowledge, and values that will make it possible for my students to change the world. *This* lesson will really make a difference! So in our self-contained classroom, we "do" social studies all day long. After all, changing the world takes time.

But it's not open-the-text, read-the-chapter, answer-the-questions-at-the-end social studies. It is integrated, active, meaningful social studies. And it is fun. Social studies is the core of our day, providing powerful learning in the humanities and social sciences for the purpose of helping children learn to be good problem solvers and wise decision makers.

I have reorganized my year with intermediate-grade children to reflect an integration of knowledge, skills, and processes. Social studies content is the thematic base around which I wrap other disciplines. Our day is unified by purposes and goals. All the components—content, instructional approaches, learning activities, and evaluation methods— are selected because they help students acquire important capabilities and dispositions. It is through the language arts that my students most often reveal their knowledge and apply their skills. Reading, writing, listening, and speaking are integral to all learning. Without language arts, the construction of meaning in specific topics is impossible. We use the natural integrative nature of language arts to promote powerful learning and teaching in the social studies.

1

REORGANIZING THE CURRICULUM

Now, nearly every part of the year is integrated in my classroom. But I didn't start that way. My initial attempts at connecting the chunks of content I was supposed to teach were clumsy, often lopsided. The revision took time. I now know integration is never finished. It starts slowly and builds over time. I've been at this for twelve years and recognize it is an evolutionary process, calling for continual refinement, as I incorporate new resources, respond to students' interests and needs, and encourage them to investigate current issues and concerns. Reorganizing the curriculum is *intensely personal and fluid*. This kind of integration will never be put in a box or a plastic bag and sold off the shelf. This kind of teaching trusts the teacher to be a good problem solver and wise decider because the teacher has a vision. This kind of teacher not only knows the likely prior knowledge and experiences of her students, but also has a good idea of what will happen next in their intellectual, social, physical, moral, and emotional development. She capitalizes on areas of strength and bolsters areas of weakness.

I began integrating in the early 1980s. Recently returned from several years of teaching in the South Pacific, I was frustrated and dismayed by the fragmentation of the school day. More demands were placed on me daily: global studies, economic education, sex education, higher-order thinking skills, personal safety, and cooperative learning. However, no time was added, no content deleted. I felt like a juggler keeping a dozen or more glass balls in the air. I knew I had already dropped a couple. Their shards lay at my feet, and there were corresponding squares in the plan book with a big X hastily crossed over them. It was also obvious that there would be new balls for me to juggle every year. Some of these balls were legislatively mandated—AIDS education and environmental awareness, for example. Others reflected concerns within my community, such as multicultural education and technology. Still others were of my own choosing: a personal interest in raising salmon in the classroom and a passion for southwest archeology.

In spite of the overwhelming demands, some days seemed to flow. The day would be over and the students and I would look at each other, astonished that we didn't have more time together. Those days were accidents of planning that integrated knowledge, skills, and processes. Over time, I realized that flow happened on those days when I hadn't taken out the teachers manual and followed what it said to do page by page, when I had ignored the sequential school-mandated, district-sanctioned, state-enforced timetable of learning: math fifty minutes daily, social studies and science forty minutes three times a week, spelling fifteen minutes right after lunch.

WHERE ARE WE GOING?

Using social studies as the framework, I began to explore ways to network knowledge, skills, and teaching strategies across the curriculum. But first I needed to know where I was going. Basically, I had twelve goals. I wanted to provide students the opportunity to

1. Learn about the past to better understand the present in order to anticipate and prepare for the future.
2. Develop an understanding of and an appreciation for our American heritage.
3. Understand the relationship between human societies and their physical world.
4. Understand how the economy and a changing workplace affect their lives now and in the future.
5. Accept the integrity and importance of the individual in the context of his or her culture and appreciate the multicultural nature of the United States and the world.
6. Understand the interdependence of their own community and the world.
7. Recognize change as a natural part of life and deal with it effectively.
8. Increase their understanding of and appreciation for systems of law.
9. Appreciate self and demonstrate respect for every human being.
10. Develop critical thinking skills.
11. Improve their individual and group communication skills.
12. Demonstrate responsible citizenship through active participation.
    (Mercer Island Public Schools)

With these overall goals, I could begin to plot a conceptual map, analyzing and reorganizing my curriculum to reach them. Twelve years ago, there wasn't a lot of help. I floundered around, doing the best I could.

POWERFUL TEACHING AND LEARNING

We currently have an excellent vehicle to move us to our destination. The National Council for the Social Studies recently issued a position statement entitled *A Vision of Powerful Teaching and Learning in the Social Studies: Building Social Understanding and Civic Efficacy*. Published in 1993, this document has tremendous implications for our classrooms because it identifies five features for ideal, or powerful, teaching and learning in the social studies. Social studies teaching and learning is powerful when it is *integrative*, *meaningful*, *value based*, *active*, and *challenging*.

These five features have enduring applicability across grade levels and content. After analyzing my own teaching, I find these five features are the essential ingredients for my classroom program, which is centered on the social studies and the purpose of which is to help students develop social understanding and civic efficacy. Social understanding is defined as "the integrated knowledge of social aspects of the human condition: how they evolved over time, the variations that occur in various physical environments and cultural settings, and the emerging trends that appear likely to shape the future." Civic efficacy is "the readiness and willingness to assume citizenship responsibilities," including social studies knowledge and skills, related values (such as concern for the common good), and dispositions (such as an orientation toward confident participation in civic affairs) (NCSS 1993, 213).

HANDS-ON, HEADS-ON, HEARTS-ON

Powerful social studies teaching requires reflective thinking and decision making as the lesson takes place. Beginning with John Dewey, curriculum advocates have called for hands-on learning. In the seventies, the notion of heads-on learning came to the fore as we examined higher-order thinking. I believe these last few years of the nineties will add a third dimension critical to learning, "hearts-on."

For years many educators skirted the affective and sought refuge in the observable. Remember? Not so long ago, learning didn't count if it couldnt be seen, touched, tasted, smelled, or heard a replicable number of times. Understanding, knowing, feeling, appreciating, caring, and loving were depreciated as attributes of learning. Yet teachers always knew the affective was not only a vital outcome, but also an important part of process.

GENUINE QUESTIONS

Teachers need to encourage students to ask genuine questions through-out the day, and teachers need to take that risk themselves. In a readers workshop session at Regis University's 1992 Literacy Institute, Patricia Hagerty, author of *Readers' Workshop: Real Reading* (1992), stated that genuine questions are those questions we don't know the answer to. We need to gain the confidence to move away from the teachers manuals, workbooks, and answer keys, not because they are bad, but because they raise nongenuine questions.

Teachers, at last, are no longer expected to be the font of all knowl-edge. Instead, we are becoming facilitators, guides, managers, mentors, and fellow learners. We share in the discourse of the classroom, enjoy the hunt for knowledge, and celebrate as our efforts culminate into a personal "whole" for each learner.

WHOLE LEARNING

Deliberately and specifically using language arts as the foundation for acquiring knowledge, skills, and values in social studies moves teachers and students to whole learning. I believe the demands of the intermediate-grade classroom push us to finding networks of knowledge and content connections beyond those found in language alone. Think of language arts skills, processes, and knowledge as the warp of learning, with each specific skill or understanding symbolized by a thread running vertically through the loom. Then picture another discipline, such as social stud-ies, as the horizontal threads providing the pattern and individuality of the fabric eventually woven by each learner. Just as whole language is a way of thinking as well as a way of doing, whole learning is a way of balancing content and instructional strategies to nurture and nudge the whole child away from self-centeredness toward self-realization and self-actualization.

INTEGRATION

The key to whole learning is integration. Integration is a concept that has been promoted by many a good educator but is illusive when one tries to pin it down. I suspect that's because integration happens in the classroom at varying levels. If one were to draw a continuum and label one end "I have a totally integrated classroom" and label the other end

"I never integrate," few teachers would identify themselves on either end. Integration in the intermediate-grade classroom can be an accidental correlation, like learning about measuring to scale in math in the morning and estimating distance on a map in the social studies text in the afternoon. It can also be as pervasive as a yearlong theme with units deliberately tied together to emphasize and elucidate that theme.

When I listen to colleagues talk about integration, I am reminded of Ed Young's wonderful book, *Seven Blind Mice* (1992), based on the fable of the blind men and the elephant. Seven blind mice venture out to examine "the Something" and each mouse comes back with a different idea. The first mouse examines only the leg and determines the something is a pillar. The second mouse examines the trunk and is sure the something is a snake. The third mouse runs up and down a tusk and decides he's found a spear. Standing on the something's head, the fourth blind mouse decides he's discovered a great cliff. The fifth mouse, perched on an ear, exclaims he's found a fan. The sixth mouse, finding the tail, concludes he's found a rope. From each individual perspective, each mouse is right. But the seventh mouse examines the whole and discovers the something is an elephant. The moral to the story? As Ed Young writes, "Knowing in part may make a fine tale, but wisdom comes from seeing the whole"(36). Isn't that true of teaching and learning? Over the years we've woven some fine tales for our students. We've created worthwhile and engaging units of study. What we've done hasn't been bad. But I believe there's more we can do; we can bring wisdom to our classrooms as well.

Our something in education is integration. And all my colleagues are right. Integration is what each individual perceives at a particular time and place. A dictionary definition of integration reveals this part-to-whole nature: "1. To make into a whole by bringing all parts together; unify 2. To join with something else; unite" (Morris 1982). Integration occurs when one thing is joined with another or when all the parts of something are unified into a whole.

TWO KINDS OF INTEGRATION

My experience tells me not one but two specific kinds of integration occur in the classroom. The first, and most obvious, is *integrating the curriculum*, what we teach. Several different approaches to curriculum integration are used successfully (Shoemaker 1991, 793):

6

- Looking for places where skills from one curriculum can be infused in another (i.e., transferring thinking skills across the curriculum).
- Identifying themes and selecting subject matter appropriate to the organizing topic (i.e., pioneers, immigration).
- Choosing concepts (i.e., interdependence, change) around which to organize a school year. (This approach is often selected when a whole school decides to begin integrating across grade levels and across curriculum.)
- Taking advantage of natural subject links (i.e., language arts and social studies).
- Establishing an integrated language arts program (connecting writing, reading, listening, and speaking).

Many teachers combine several of these approaches, customizing integration to fit their curriculum goals and the resources available.

The second, more subtle kind of integration focuses on the needs and strengths of the whole child. This occurs when we specifically consider and plan for the continued development of the *cognitive, physical, affective, and moral dimensions of each child* (793), carefully devising learning strategies to deepen and extend his or her arena of competence, confidence, creativity, and cooperation. It is here that knowing our students, being aware of their learning orientation and prior experiences, begins to fuse with curriculum. The way we emphasize content, how it is presented, and how it is developed through activities is incredibly important. It is this fusion of the child, the curriculum, and our teaching that results in whole learning. Only then can wisdom enter our classroom.

ANALOGICAL THINKING

Integration calls upon the teacher, initially, and later the students to identify the connections or overlaps between content areas, between similar processes or applications of skills, and then to build upon those connections. Don Bragaw (1986), former National Council for the Social Studies president, identifies this ability as "analogical thinking." He calls it the ultimate form of critical thinking, "that moment when a student responds in class by saying, Hey, that's like when so and so did whatzis back in the Civil War (or the Renaissance, or in economics class, or in third grade, or in a book they just read, or in a classroom discussion held just yesterday)." Integration encourages the learner to draw on observations and resources from art, drama, poetry, and music. When learning is rooted firmly in the social studies, meaningfulness is enhanced. Children develop the skills and attitudes, as well as the knowledge, to be able to participate in the decision making that is basic to a democratic system.

As one's comfort with integration grows, the connections become larger than a topic, more global than a theme, and—in the intermediate grades—last longer than a day. Centered on the child, connected by the curriculum. driven by learning goals, and encompassing the amount of time the teacher and the students spend together, the threads of content continue to interweave with the skills of communication, the patterns of problem solving, and the synthesis of decision making over an entire school year.

After three to five years of continued practice, teachers who seek to integrate will find more and more ways to connect curriculum, until they discover, as I did, that the day is overstuffed with connections. It's not a disaster. It's like winning the lottery. Now there are options. Students can choose how they want to approach a question, explore a topic, or develop a plan. Enough material and approaches have been collected and connected to encourage individualization within whole learning.

LEVELS OF INTEGRATION

Many of us start integrating by deliberately making connections across the curriculum. That is how I started out. This kind of approach is often referred to as interdisciplinary. I took traditional subjects—social studies, language arts (including reading), science, and art—and found those places where content could intersect, where skills could be applied across the curriculum. While social studies was the core for me, other teachers have used science, math, or some other subject as the core organizer.

Looking back, I can trace four levels of integration in my teaching.

Level 1
Connections were few, rather formal, and carefully planned the first year. The question I repeatedly asked myself was, How can I connect this reading content, that writing skill, an art perspective to my existing social studies curriculum? Because I was new to the grade level, new

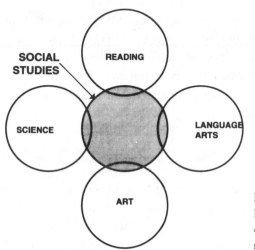

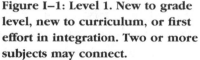
Figure I–1: Level 1. New to grade level, new to curriculum, or first effort in integration. Two or more subjects may connect.

to the curriculum, and new to integrating, I had to seek out every connection. I didn't have many connections that first year (see Figure I–1). Picking content I had a personal interest and knowledge in helped, because I didn't have to start from scratch. It helps to know something about what you're trying to connect!

Level 2
A couple of years later, my planning became less formal but broader in scope, blending skills and content through the disciplines. The question I now asked myself was, How can I blend this social studies concept with those skills with these learning strategies of reading, writing, science, and art? I began to use the connections to weave the disciplines together, to connect subjects in a new way (see Figure I–2). I believe

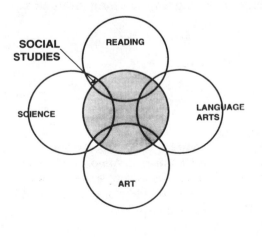

Figure I–2: Level 2. Greater familiarization with curriculum, student's development, resources, and activities that work weave multiple connections.

this shift occurred because I was more familiar with the curriculum and could identify a larger number of resources to support it. I was getting smarter about the central content (social studies) and ways to teach it. I was also getting better at knowing what my students would probably know and not know. I could anticipate and plan for their understanding and misunderstanding.

Level 3

I call this level highly integrated. Planning in an inclusive, integrative manner became not only natural, but essential: I no longer viewed learning as a mixture of separate subjects. I knew the curriculum intimately and was well aware of resources within the school and throughout the community. I knew where the class and I were going and I had created or adapted teaching strategies to get there. Subjects began to fuse as the new patterns of teaching and learning became established. Discipline identity was no longer the focus (see Figure I–3).

Level 4

Recently, I have noticed a fourth level in my personal evolution of integration. In the past, the focus, or center, of my integrating was always the topic, the theme, or the concept. But I've realized that teaching a series of disconnected units, no matter how integrated each unit is, does not tap the potential power of integration in the classroom. My organizational center has shifted. The child, not the subject, is now at the center of my planning (see Figure I–4).

Why has this happened? Partly, I suspect, it's because of the shift in the way learning and schooling are being thought about: they aren't something teachers do to kids. Children come to school with prior knowledge and experiences. Finally, though, it's because I have been deliberately developing integrative teaching and learning strategies. I

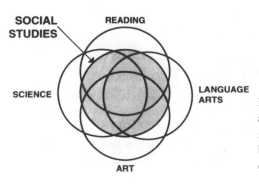

Figure I–3: Level 3. Highly accomplished. Almost all learning intersects as subject distinctions begin to blur. Concepts and skills cross disciplines.

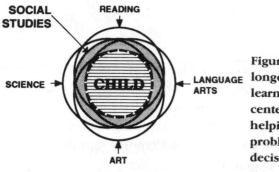

Figure I–4: Level 4. Subjects no longer drive learning. Instead, learning is a meaningful child-centered, holistic experience helping children become good problem solvers and wise decision makers.

have multiple ways to provide individual students opportunities to apply skills across the curriculum, to explore content from many perspectives, and to examine their own feelings and attitudes as well as be aware of conflicting values. Having a repertoire of strategies to draw on makes personalized teaching possible. Being able to offer students a wide spectrum of ways to demonstrate what they know, what they can do, and how they feel fosters individual growth and development. Learning is personally meaningful.

I've also observed that I function on several different levels of integration within a school year. Let me give you an example. I know a great deal about Northwest Coastal Indians. I have studied the culture for years and continue to expand my knowledge. When we focus on Northwest Coastal Indians in my classroom, I easily and effectively make connections with everything else we do during the day. Finding appropriate materials, devising substantial projects, and facilitating the students' individual investigations is stress free. I know the content. I know the kids. I have collected a wide variety of strategies and resources to enhance learning.

But *integration is not linear*. Just because I have this facility with Northwest Coastal Indians does not mean that all the work and planning for the rest of the year is equally accomplished. I would categorize integration during our Civil War studies as a Level 2. Content, my knowledge of the issues and events, is not as substantial as it could be. The classroom resources aren't as rich and diverse as I'd like. Similarly, the level of integration reached during our study of explorers is a Level 1, because only recently have accurate and engaging resources started to appear that present data from different points of view in easily accessible formats for intermediate-age students. Resources, knowledge of the content, and an array of teaching strategies are essential elements upon which to build higher levels of integration.

ABOUT THIS BOOK

When NCSS (National Council for the Social Studies) published *A Vision of Powerful Teaching and Learning in the Social Studies*, I analyzed my teaching and my students' learning by comparing the *Vision* to my classroom. This book grew out of that analysis and my own journey toward a classroom in which learning is integrated for the benefit of the whole child. Frequently, the strategies I employ and the learning going on in my classroom match the *Vision*. Sometimes they don't.

This book chronicles a twelve-year period of my life and reflects a variety of integration levels, sometimes within the same chapter. However, social studies remains the core. Whether learning is highly integrated or barely connected, today's students must interact with worthwhile content in a meaningful way, so that they "develop the ability to make informed and reasoned decisions for the public good as citizens of a culturally diverse, democratic society in an interdependent world (NCSS, 1993, 213)."

I use a fifth-grade classroom to show what a social studies–integrated curriculum looks like over a year's time. A few years ago, I would have organized this book in separate chapters, illustrating the in-depth study of a theme, topic, or issue. It's only recently that integration has moved to a more holistic level for me. Things we do in January and in March relate to and build on knowledge, skills, and ideas we explored in September. Substantive underlying concepts and a yearlong theme bridge my teaching, day by day, throughout the year. Moving the child to the center of the curriculum has added a deeper layer of understanding for me and for my students.

How content is presented and how it is developed through activities is as important as what is presented. I'm constantly seeking to balance the message and the medium. Too much process and an activity becomes "cute." Intermediate-age children need substance. Too little process and learning becomes a drudge. Intermediate-age children need to be engaged in learning to excel. We need to choose strategies that create an active, child-centered classroom where students expose and explore critical content.

Children need to deepen their reservoirs of knowledge. And they need the opportunity to dip into that knowledge, blend it with the ability to solve problems and make good decisions in developmentally appropriate ways. This book is about reorganizing curriculum and choosing instructional strategies to make learning integrative, meaningful, value-based, active, and challenging for both the students and the teacher. It is also about one teacher's quest for the balance that brings wholeness to learning, for her students and for herself.

The chapters that follow illustrate how social studies concepts, issues, and themes can become the core of the intermediate-grade day. Language arts, art, science, and math can be gradually interwoven to integrate learning in any intermediate-grade classroom. Teachers can intentionally capitalize on the connections between subjects and among processes to strengthen their teaching and increase learning.

Detailed plans for many of the strategies are included in the appendix, with the hope readers will take them, shape them, and integrate them into their own classrooms. While I don't use all of these strategies in any one year, I believe they are all useful and versatile. My students find them appealing. And these same strategies have been successfully used by elementary and middle school teachers in a variety of subjects to teach a number of topics, themes, and concepts.

Throughout the book I also share read-alouds, those picture books and chapter books I read to my students, and read-alones, those books I either recommend or require my students read as a part of our integrated approach to learning.

Chapter 1, Making Connections

This chapter offers a historical perspective of my own journey to seeing the whole. Sometimes, knowing the path someone else has taken can save time and energy or affirm that we are, in fact, on a path that leads to "something."

Chapter 2, Setting Up for Success

Starting off positively and productively affects learning dynamics for a whole year. Some procedures and strategies seem to promote a more successful year in our classroom than others do. This chapter presents underpinnings that enhance and encourage student learning and participation.

Chapter 3, Implementing Integration

What does integration in the intermediate-grade classroom look like when social studies is the center? This chapter provides classroom vignettes and specific teaching strategies you can use in your classroom tomorrow.

Chapter 4, Making It Meaningful

This chapter reaches to the heart of teaching. At the intermediate level our students not only have to learn how to learn, they also have to learn something. Determining issues worth spending time on and devising activities of substance, while at the same time developing lifelong learners is all a part of making learning full of meaning.

Chapter 5, Exploring Values and Points of View
Helping our students gain an understanding of and an appreciation for multiple perspectives is critical. Being aware of how our own values affect our selection of materials and the amount of time we choose to spend on a topic helps us provide a balanced program for our students. This chapter clearly illustrates strategies and activities for making multiple perspectives real.

Chapter 6, Activating Learning
Moving students beyond the classroom walls, both literally and figuratively, brings learning to life. Authentic learning in the form of thinking, feeling, and doing energizes the learner and the learning. By actively constructing meaning, students are able to apply it to their lives. This chapter focuses on how to make learning active without losing substance or skills.

Chapter 7, Making Teaching and Learning Challenging
Developing a learning community in which each member of the class is challenged to meet a high level of understanding and a depth of purpose takes time, and the teacher needs to offer a model. This chapter shows how thoughtful discussion and the practice of thinking skills, both critical and creative, contribute to seeing the whole.

Chapter 8, Accenting Assessment
Grades, student-created criteria, peer critiques, and projects of excellence are all part of my quest to authenticate assessment. This final chapter offers some ideas and strategies for looking at assessment in an integrated classroom.

Chapter One

MAKING CONNECTIONS

THERE ARE MANY CONNECTIONS BETWEEN
WORTHWHILE CONTENT AND EFFECTIVE PROCESS.
—NCSS's *Vision*

THE BEGINNING

It all began quite intentionally. My colleague Jan Hoem and I were
convinced that if we started putting things together in our classrooms,
the world could become a better place. In the early eighties, we were
given a minigrant from our school district to do just that. The grant
didn't specifically state that we were to change the world, of course,
but it underwrote planning time in which to reorganize our fifth-grade
curriculum to increase student learning. We read somewhere that American Indian children tend to learn better in a holistic classroom. We
weren't sure what this meant, but it sounded better than the fragmented
curriculum we were juggling each day: kibbles of content, bits of skills,
pieces of predetermined information taught in a sequence ordered by
someone who had never seen our classroom, never met our students,
never asked what we thought. Since an American Indian child would
be in my classroom in the fall and because Jan and I team planned, we
were given Title IV funds to support our efforts.

Jan taught fifth grade next door to me. She is one of those "born"
teachers. Always curious, ever alert, incredibly sensitive, Jan gave of
herself in ways that inspired me to be a better person. A poet, a pragma-
tist, and a good friend, she was frustrated by too little time and too
much content. I agreed and added my pet peeves of too much rote and
too little active learning. We talked many times about finding ways to
challenge the able kids and ways to enable the challenged kids. Teaching
in those days was presented as series of sequential student objectives

that limited learning to a single, narrow focus. We weren't happy with boring workbooks, "pretend" writing, or dull textbooks. We searched for ways to take the isolation out of our basal readers. Learning was fragmented, generalizations rare, motivation sporadic. We were determined to do something about it. Both of us knew learning could be fun, because we had fun learning ourselves. We got excited about solving problems. Why didn't our students?

So, on a hot August day, we agreed that we were going to try to reorganize our curriculum in a way that would bring cohesiveness to the school day and meet childrens' needs as best we could anticipate. We wanted to make thinking fundamental in our classroom studies, to reach beyond the standard text and workbook format for more creative ways to teach and learn. And, because both of us loved social studies more than any other subject, we wanted to use it as the center of our curriculum. An analysis of social studies convinced us that social studies was a solid core for organizing our learning.

SOCIAL STUDIES INTEGRATES NATURALLY

Social studies is about life. It is a naturally integrative subject. Look at all the pieces that are frequently included in a K–12 social studies strand: anthropology, archeology, civics, economics, geography, government, history, political science, psychology, religion, sociology, ethnic studies, global education, law-related education. It has a richness to draw from that promotes multilevel thinking. Children need not start from recall or memory in social studies. They can move directly to analysis, synthesis, and problem solving, depending on whether the task is to form a group, develop an argument for one side of an engaging issue, or create a plan of action.

SOCIAL STUDIES ACCOMODATES LEARNING STYLES

Social studies is so diverse that it invites the learner to explore content through many different avenues. For example, a historical document like the Bill of Rights can be studied through singing, dancing, writing, drawing, debating, and deliberating. A few years after we had begun our first attempts at integration, Dr. Howard Gardner published *Frames of Mind* (1985), in which he identified multiple intelligences. Jan and I were aware that children could show what they knew in many ways but hadn't ever deliberately planned to tap into these multiple intelligences. Dr. Gardner's work has become a useful intellectual tool for

During our hobby fair, Katie introduces us to her love of faraway places.

planning and talking about integration. So often research comes to us in the classroom this way. We do things because we know they are good for kids, but we haven't articulated why. Researchers like Dr. Gardner help us understand why the things we do work. I make a deliberate effort to plan learning activities that provide opportunities for all children to deepen and extend the ways in which they learn. I often use Dr. Gardner's multiple intelligences as a way to guide my choices of teaching strategies and learning activities. He describes them this way (Campbell 1989):

LINGUISTICALLY ORIENTED STUDENTS

Love language: speaking it, hearing it, reading it, writing it
Often have well-developed vocabularies
Demonstrate rich expression, elaboration, fluency
Do not avoid difficult reading material
Like to work with books, records, and tapes

INTERPERSONALLY ORIENTED LEARNERS

Enjoy learning by interaction
Like cooperating with others
Are eager to participate in group work
Respond to discussions
Are interested in how peers feel about classwork
Get involved in clubs, community service
Desire to know social relevancy of learning activities
Enjoy all kinds of social activities

INTRAPERSONALLY ORIENTED LEARNERS

Are self-directed
Are independent
Enjoy quiet times
Like private places to work and reflect
Need opportunities to fantasize, dream, imagine
Are concerned about the meaning of life
Look for personal relevance and purpose
Benefit from processing feelings
Need to solve problems

VISUALLY/SPATIALLY ORIENTED LEARNERS

Love learning with images, pictures, charts, graphs, diagrams, and art
Enjoy films, slides, videos, maps, models

Often arrive at unique solutions
Are willing to experiment
Do not rely on traditional approaches

KINESTHETICALLY ORIENTED LEARNERS

Learn best by moving, touching, doing
Need short movement breaks
Enjoy all kinds of hands-on activities
Find multisensory experiences appealing
Are often not attentive to visual or auditory instruction
Remember best what they have done physically

LOGICALLY/MATHEMATICALLY ORIENTED STUDENTS

Enjoy forming concepts
Like looking for patterns and relationships
Are comfortable doing activities step-by-step
Like proceeding in a sequential manner
Need the time to complete all the steps
Enjoy experimenting with new materials
Frequently ask many questions
Desire logical explanations
Think games, kits, and puzzles are fun

MUSICALLY ORIENTED LEARNERS

Enjoy rhythm and melody
Learn easily when information is sung, tapped, or clapped out
Like to listen to music as they work
Enjoy using instruments
Like attending musical performances
Seek out opportunities to create music.

SOCIAL STUDIES FOSTERS MULTICULTURAL/ GLOBAL EDUCATION

Social studies engages the learner personally in recognizing and valuing differences and similarities. It is inclusive, putting what is familiar to students into historical, geographical, and cultural perspectives. It enlarges the narrow vision students frequently have of their immediate society, one they may take for granted without much awareness or appreciation. Teaching students about diverse points of view and fostering appreciation for cultural differences is easier when the whole day revolves around social studies concepts and themes. The very process of the democratic classroom, where all members are valued and respected and there is an absence of threat, is the foundation of multicultural global education.

SOCIAL STUDIES PROMOTES FLOW

Using social studies as the core of the day promotes flow. Flow occurs in the classroom when the day's activities are a cohesive and productive whole. Practicing skills from language arts such as writing a friendly letter or a newspaper article fits authentically within a social studies framework. Why should children have to generate a make-believe topic for a newspaper article when they can create a Civil War newspaper as a culminating activity for their study of the Civil War? Why should they struggle over a friendly letter to a nonexistent person when they can be Pocahontas writing to her father from England? Knowledge, skills, beliefs, and values are all revealed in assignments like these. They fit, like giant puzzle pieces. Students are given time to assemble analogies, to find the Hey, Mrs. L., isn't that just like . . . ? They are given time to mix knowledge and process into a workable whole for themselves. At the end of the day, there is a sense of accomplishment and closure. It is the kind of satisfied feeling that makes everyone want to rub their hands together, place them on their hips, and survey the job well done. Over the years, we discovered flow can be planned. It can be predicted and directed as we consciously connect significant content, skills, and perspectives from a variety of disciplines to create essential learning experiences. Learning for the whole child, every child, is not only possible, but powerful.

SOCIAL STUDIES VALUES TIME

Although we didn't realize it when we first started connecting skills, knowledge, and processes across the curriculum, I have since learned that when the children read a historical novel, like *The Double Life of Pocahontas* (Fritz 1983), write about it, and compare it to the data given in the social studies textbook, they recognize that their time is valued and valuable. They recognize the deliberate layering of learning. They become aware of the validity of the assignment. No longer do assignments seem arbitrary and capricious. No longer are they rushed from one small segment of study to another. No longer does the teacher hear a chorus of, Do we have to? Time is allowed for initial study, knowledge application, and reflection—by both the children and the teacher.

And time is a key factor in today's classroom. Finding the time to track the important ideas of social studies *after* reading, writing, listening, and speaking is usually a scramble for minutes instead of the hours needed for in-depth study. By reorganizing the curriculum and devising teaching strategies so that social studies content becomes the center of language arts practice and enjoyment, intermediate-grade teachers can find the precious time needed to teach their students not only what they need to know, but new ways of knowing it. Students are able to become more engaged in learning. They aren't just covering a subject. Instead they are excavating, exploring, and examining it. By integrating the day around social studies, the teacher gains time and so do the students. Time is used most effectively and efficiently when content is linked with skills. For example, when the teacher doesn't create a whole new setup for a friendly letter but suggests that the students recall, as Pocahontas, her stay in England, and when students don't need to take ten minutes to decide whom to write to, time can be spent on the quality of the letter and the depth of comprehension in the writer's portrayal of Pocahantas's feelings.

We began to create strategies to strengthen the links across the curriculum. From the beginning, we used language arts skills to showcase social studies knowledge. We found we seldom needed to have a formal language arts period, because those skills were applied during the integrated block. Practice, models, and critiques helped firm up language arts skills within a social studies context.

SOCIAL STUDIES COMBINES BREADTH AND DEPTH

We wanted the curriculum we created to be more authentic and more productive. Our planning strategy was to reorganize after first identifying where current content touched (see Figure 1–1). We knew we couldn't do it all in one year, but we could begin. (See page 164 in the appendix for a recent yearlong plan.)

We identified the broad topics that we wanted the students to learn about: First Peoples, exploration, colonization, American Indians with a Northwest Coastal emphasis, the Revolution and documents of democracy, the westward movement, the Civil War, immigration, and industrialization. We wanted to study these topics broadly and deeply. In-depth studies provide the time and intensity needed for students to construct a thorough understanding of important concepts, acquire skills and

1988-1989	Reading/L.A.	Social Studies	Science	Art	Other
September	Stories, factual articles, folktales, biographies from other cultures / Time lines / Artifacts / Newspapers	Immigrants / Map and globe skills	Focus on Social Studies	Folk tale Story boards / chops / Daruma-San / Multicultural posters & post cards	Jamaica Drive "Hurricane Gilbert" / Me Book
October	"We"-search reports, / Reader's theatre / Letters to consulates / poetry	China / Korea / Pacific Rim introduction	Moon study distance gravity position conditions	Shadow puppets / Crafts / Origami	World Hunger Day / U.N. Day / International Bazaar / International Potluck
November	Novels on American colonization & Revolutionary War period	Colonization of America - physical geographical political economic	Geology - sediments plates erosion fossils rocks	Patterns and Quilts / Geometric designs / Colonial crafts	"Johnny Tremain" / Oral biographies
December	Famous Americans, founding fathers - other perspectives	Revolutionary War period & study of the Constitution	Winds convection causes relationship to weather speed velocity	Early American reproductions - artists & artisans	Rube Goldberg Day
January	Folk tales, stories & legends of N.W. Native Americans / Speech as an elder	Land bridge theory / Eskimos & N.A. of Alaska / Pacific NW Native Americans	Classification of plants & animals / Interdependence food chains	Reproducing NW coastal art - line form pattern / Chilkat blanket	Artifacts from Burke museum / Poo Putsch on Navajo
February March	Endangered Species reports / Stories of children during different periods in Am. history.	Civil War / Reconstruction / Industrialization	Sea life of Puget Sound / Pollution	Books about sea life / Murals	Aquarium on Wheels
April	Stories to do w/ self concept, handicaps & disabilities / Advertising techniques	Focus on science	The Human Body - all systems, plus Safety Nutrition Self Esteem	Posters - design & layout / Diagram of Body systems	Field trips
May June	Science Fiction and fantasy. read write create plays	Constitutional Visions - creating a space colony 100 years in the future	Drug & Alcohol Education / Refusal skills / Matter & Energy	Analyze ad-color layout / Create costumes for the future / Design space colony	Field trips / Fifth Grade event / Healthy Deli

Figure 1–1: An early yearlong integrated plan with social studies at the center.

knowledge, and explore values. We felt that each of these topics was significantly important to developing a historical understanding of our country. We also felt they were broad enough to encourage generalizations across content. These topics allowed us to choose from a variety of organizing themes: conflict and cooperation, continuity and change, community, power, unity and diversity, justice, civic virtue, or liberty.

We saw we could spend about a month on each topic, maybe five weeks here, six weeks there. Or we could hurry up with some topics and really dive into another for an extended period. It is the balance between breadth and depth that requires good teaching judgment. It felt good to contemplate the number of days we would have for social studies, not minutes or hours.

ESTABLISHING READING CONNECTIONS

The easiest link for us to develop was between social studies and reading. First, we decided the textbook would be another resource, not the whole curriculum. We observed that when the textbook is used as the sole source for social studies education, students are often turned off by its stale, static, and impersonal presentation. Second, we knew that intermediate-age students needed to add a new and important skill to their reading repertoire, the skill of reading to learn. They needed frequent practice reading factual material. They needed to summarize, analyze, synthesize, and realize their own potential as "data navigators" (Winbury 1993).

We also knew that reading to learn needed to be balanced with reading literature. Back in the early eighties, no one I knew was talking about whole language. Basals, with the teacher reading aloud after recess, were the state of the art in reading instruction. Literature was something that happened in high school. Since the order of stories in basals has no significance whatsoever, we looked through all the old fourth-, fifth-, and sixth-grade reading series to find stories that enriched, extended, or enhanced the concepts we were studying in social studies. Then we added novels. We encouraged the students to try many different kinds of printed material.

That first year, we chose stories from the basal that connected in some way to our topics. Where there were none, we found literature to read aloud. We shared magazine and newspaper articles. Sometimes the students created their own textbook. Later, we developed lists of books students could read independently that examined, extended, or enriched our specific social studies topics. By saving book coupons from various book clubs and by pooling coupons with other teachers, we acquired sets of books to share. (Today, I use a reading workshop approach. For one hour a day, we do reading-related activities. Basically, the first half hour is spent silent reading. The next half hour is divided between journal writing and class sharing.)

The public library system is also an excellent resource. Ours is a countywide system, with many libraries networked together. By placing an "all call" for a specific title, fifteen to twenty copies of a single title or a collection of related books are often available within a week. Grant money can also bring books into the classroom. My most successful grant came when I explained how I was integrating my curriculum around social studies themes and concepts and why I needed literature to support that effort. The result? About two hundred social studies–related literature books for our classroom library! Over the years, the basal has been replaced by historical fiction, biographies, picture books, and factual material. It has taken ten years to build a personal library that supports fifth-grade teaching and learning. Each year my library grows, as new books are published connecting content and teaching goals and as resources are found to buy them.

ALIGNING LANGUAGE ARTS CONNECTIONS

After identifying stories to read, we connected language arts skills by linking them through activities related to the reading. We looked at the school district's list of skills and objectives for language arts. We thought about our students' skills, abilities, and interests. It was not difficult to weave together language arts skills and social studies content: letters, news articles, speeches, poetry, outlines, and other forms of written and spoken communication are all wonderful tools. In fact, we wondered why we hadn't intentionally done this before. We both recognized that successful past projects were a blend of language arts and social studies, but it had been accidental!

In addition to the district goals, we had some personal ones. For instance, we wanted our students to do more expository writing. We felt they needed to move from writing narratives to organizing facts in an informational or persuasive way. Students at this age have a highly developed sense of justice. We decided that studying issues, whether current or historical, would capture their interest. Various points of view can be recognized as students begin to wrestle with the reality that there is seldom a single side to any issue. We decided to teach the students how to make hypotheses and to find proof. We wanted to give them practice in choosing the best alternative and supporting that choice with facts. We provided opportunities for them to "try on" past and current decisions and to evaluate actual or potential consequences.

Listening with a critical ear is a skill preadolescents need, given that they are plugged in to, glued to, and centered on music, radio, video games, and television. Learning to discriminate fallacious arguments, weak substance, and shaky premises increases their street smarts as well as helps them acquire intellectual skills. The persistent dilemmas and issues of social studies provides excellent forums for practicing critical listening.

This age group teeters on the brink of public-speaking phobia. Increasingly more concerned about their public image, many of them find speaking before a group an ordeal. Yet public speaking is becoming an ordinary way to share information or to persuade. Talk shows abound on radio and television. Public meetings for airing grievances, identifying problems, and discussing alternative solutions vie for spots on the community calendar. With frequent practice in a variety of settings, intermediate-age students can gain competence and confidence in their ability to contribute orally in any context. Conducting mock trials, simulating public meetings, or creating persuasive ads to sway public opinion about a historical event are just a few of standard social studies strategies we decided to use.

SEEKING SCIENCE CONNECTIONS

After carefully connecting reading and language arts to our social studies curriculum, we looked at our science curriculum. We were expected to teach the moon, classification of plants and animals, earth science, flight, and movement of air. We decided to connect the moon with explorers, since it seemed to us that if we were exploring the earth, then we could look at the sky as well. We didn't intentionally integrate. We simply placed the moon activities and content adjacent to our primary study of explorers.

Flight and movement of air fit together naturally. We decided to place it at the end of immigration. Using Laurence Yep's *Dragonwings* (1975), we segued from Chinese American life to airplanes and extended it with an independent study of inventions. Earth science fit nicely with Inuit studies. Classification of plants and animals felt right with American Indians.

A favorite classroom activity: watching our salmon grow.

WHY NOT MATH?

Jan and I decided that first year that we wouldn't attempt to integrate math. We thought that finding ways to productively connect social studies, science, language arts, reading, and art would be enough. After trying to make up story problems that had a cultural motif, we decided it took more time than it was worth. In fifth grade there are specific math skills we simply have to teach. Integrating them doesn't make this teaching or learning easier. Long division needs to be analyzed and learned. Application—that is, integration—comes a bit later.

In retrospect, I think it was a good decision. Even today, I do not fully integrate the math curriculum into the rest of the day. I start the day with math, and then the rest of day spins together in a web of content, concepts, and skills. I still need to teach math directly. Ten years ago I could find no particular payoff in integrating math computation. It seemed to me that the easiest and fastest way to teach those skills was simply to teach them and move on. We found we often used math processes and computation skills during other times of the day but the initial teaching happened outside the context of the integrated curriculum. That's still true. My students *apply* mathematical content, concepts, and skills naturally in context of what they are doing. They practice math in realistic settings based on need, whether it's using a ruler to set up a quilt square, figuring the mean, mode, and median to analyze data collected in a class survey, determining how many pages they've read on the average, or wondering about the probability of history repeating itself. But I don't turn myself or my math program upside down just to integrate. Early on, I was uncomfortable with math, doubting my ability to reorganize and not foul up the learning. So I did the easy thing, I shut math out. Not any more. While seldom the focus, math is a valued tool for thinking, organizing, and problem solving.

ATTACHING ART CONNECTIONS

Next we connected the arts to our curriculum reorganization. Jan and I wanted to add music, movement, voice, acting, and visual arts. Giving

Patrick, Matt, and Peter create plants for the understory of our own classroom rain forest.

the music teacher a copy of our yearlong plan accomplished more than we imagined. She began to connect the music of America with our study of American history. She introduced the students to popular songs of the periods we were studying. She had the students dance the minuet and the reel. American composers and uniquely American music, like jazz, were listened to and talked about.

In our classrooms, we taught Chinese shadow puppet theater and studied calligraphy with the help of a local artisan as we discussed Asian immigration. We borrowed artifacts from museums and individuals. Native crafts people came into our classroom to demonstrate their expertise. Art history and art appreciation added new dimensions to classroom learning. With the help of some parents, we developed six art appreciation classes, using a chronological exploration of American artists. Since we were teaching about intellectual perspectives, it seemed reasonable to teach visual perspective from an artist's point of view.

Providing models of art projects really helps children, especially if you don't feel particularly gifted in art. I've also learned that having students analyze the form as well as talk about what is effective, what gets in the way, what intrigues them, and what puzzles them helps create a finer product. Mostly, quality artwork of any kind by children takes time. If it truly is worth doing, then providing the time for it is essential. The integrated approach makes finding that time possible.

Students don't like junk. How many times have we seen papers handed back only to be tossed in the garbage or dropped on the ground on the way home? But some pieces, precious pieces, are carefully safe-guarded and proudly displayed. One dramatic aspect of integrating art around social studies is that students have a context for their art. They aren't expected to turn on an artistic self at a specified time each week for a limited number of minutes. Instead, the art they do is an intellectual and graphic extension of their knowledge. It is another way of knowing.

MAKING REAL-WORLD CONNECTIONS

Finally, we scheduled field trips and guest speakers. We were deter-mined to have some civic action projects in the year, still based on our social studies content. Field trips to local museums to view Northwest Coastal Indian artifacts and speakers from other countries to enhance our immigration studies were pretty predictable. But having our stu-dents work with the PTA to get a street adjacent to the school declared a dead end by the city council so our school children would be safe grew out of a real need preceived by the students and their parents.

The social studies–integrated classroom provides many opportunities for students to formulate, define, and investigate problems that are important to them and their communities. They learn to value an informed approach and reasoned decisions based on what is important to their lives. By placing concepts and generalizations in past, present, and future contexts, students learn to analyze, interpret, and use information. They have the opportunity to examine recurring issues and dilemmas. They actively practice citizenship at developmentally appropriate levels through this kind of classroom. It might be choosing to sponsor a clothing drive for flood victims. It could be writing letters to a congresswoman about why the government should require double-hulled oil tankers. It might be spending lunch hours trying to solve the problem of inappropriate language on the playground. For learning to be realized, it has to be real.

NO SINGLE RIGHT WAY

The longer I live, the more I am convinced that there is no single right way to integrate. Like the mice in Ed Young's fable, each of us "sees" the whole based on our own experience and knowledge. The first-year teacher at any grade level will make connections much differently from the teacher who has been teaching the same grade, in the same district, for several years. Goals can guide the novice teacher as well as the seasoned professional, providing an initial target and a final evaluation. Knowledge of and comfort with the curriculum, the developmental level of the students, and collections of resources impact the number and substance of the connections. Probably more significant, the ways of knowing demonstrated by the kinds of activities the students have to choose from will be much richer if the teacher has had the opportunity to develop a "history" in that grade level.

There is certainly no single right way to do this kind of connecting. I'm not sure it can be mandated. Districts can develop in their instructional staff a disposition toward integration. Districts can identify integration as a worthwhile and desirable process. Districts can encourage inservice education and support by providing both time and money. But districts must remember that overall, each teacher's teaching style, passions, and values affect the connections that will be identified and fostered in individual classrooms. Integration has to make some kind of sense to the teacher. If the connection, no matter how tenuous, does make sense, then I will find ways to reveal that integration to my students, or, as I continue to discover, the students will bring it to my attention (Hey, Mrs. L., isn't that just like . . . ?).

REFLECTIONS

That was our first year. That was the first level of integration, some of the time. We connected our curriculum, sort of. It didn't go perfectly. Our focus was more on content than it was on the child. We worried more about what we were going to teach than whom we were teaching. We didn't always stick to the time lines we had set up. We didn't provide the time we had promised we would for art projects. Science integration was minimal. In fact, I hardly taught any science at all that first year.

But, teaching felt good. All the children learned. Gone were the bits of skills and the kibbles of concepts. There was a hopefulness and positiveness that permeated our relationships with others in the class. It seemed that discipline was easier.

Every year since, integration in my classroom has become more together, stronger, and more exciting. Now I know that integration can never be complete. For me, it is an ever-evolving, intensely personal balancing act. It is balancing content with process, the group with the individual, personal growth with academics, curriculum with community demands, and teacher fulfillment with district requirements. Integration makes my classroom more challenging and more fun every year as I try to bring learning to life through curriculum connected to each child.

Over the years, my fifth-grade curriculum has changed. We've embraced technology and participate in worldwide computer networks. Video cameras have opened up new ways of research, new ways to approach drama. Math has become much easier to connect naturally as we've moved from a computation-based program to a conceptual orientation. All in all, centering the day on social studies themes, concepts, and knowledge has weathered well. It is still the core of my day, the essential integrator. I'm still excited about teaching and being with children as they learn, grow, and explore. I'm learning to trust myself more and to leave the teachers manuals on the shelf. They have become resources rather than daily lesson plans.

Jan moved to another part of the state after our first couple of years, and I still miss her. Our team planning and collegial relationship helped us both grow. We talked about what worked and what didn't. We brainstormed, often piggybacking on each other's ideas to create better ways to get where we wanted to go. I think what we shared was special, and I know I wouldn't be this far along in my quest for whole learning without her. I really like what has happened to my students and to me. They come to school each day eager and ready to learn—and so do I. They don't whine or complain about the work we do—and neither do I. They ask questions, treat each other kindly, and care about the world. I do too!

Chapter Two

SETTING UP FOR SUCCESS

TEACHER-STUDENT INTERACTION
IS THE HEART OF EDUCATION,

—NCSS's *Vision*

PROMOTING COMMON GOOD

I am more convinced than ever that social studies is what schooling is truly about. While knowing facts and figures, being able to spell, read, write, and do arithmetic, are incredibly important, there are greater goals for education. One is the ability to work well with others. Another is to make thoughtful, reasoned decisions. A third is to be a good neighbor. Yet another is to be a good listener, to be able to discern more than one point of view. When community members meet today to identify the learner outcomes they want for the children in their communities, they use words and phrases like *capable, a good communicator, productive*, and *citizen in a global community*. The concept of the common good's being the responsibility of each student often underlies these descriptions.

DEFINING SOCIAL STUDIES

This emphasis on the outcome of education is reinforced by the definition of social studies as stated by the National Council for the Social Studies:

> Social studies is the integrated study of the social sciences and the humanities to promote civic competence. Within the school program, social studies provides coordinated, systematic study drawing upon such disciplines as anthropology, archaeology, geography, history, law, philosophy, political sci-

ence, psychology, religion, and sociology, as well as appropriate content from the humanities, mathematics, and natural sciences. The primary purpose of social studies is to help young people develop the ability to make informed and reasoned decisions for the public good as citizens of a culturally diverse, democratic society in an interdependent world. (NCSS 1993, 213)

LEARNING SOCIAL STUDIES ALL DAY LONG

I am equally convinced that social studies happens all day long. It begins with the morning greetings and continues through the remainder of the day, however it's structured. Issues of governance are crucial to the school day. I suspect more is learned about the real meaning of democracy, freedom, and justice in the first three days of school, before the social studies textbook is even opened, than is taught the rest of the year.

The ways in which the teacher and the class organize the room, set up protocol, and manage the classroom are vital pieces of learning that many teachers overlook. Human organization is crucial to developing civic competence. One teacher may arrange the desks in straight rows and put a name on each desk before the first day of school. Another may follow the suggestion made by Priscilla Lynch (1992): "Leave all the supplies, materials, and books stacked in the room. Don't hang up one piece of commercial poster or border. In fact, don't hang anything. When the kids come in and look like they've obviously come to the wrong room, welcome them by saying, Hi, I'm glad you're here. We've got some decisions to make!'" Most of us fall somewhere in between these two approaches.

I want my students to know, the first day they walk into my classroom, that I value group work and I value them. When they walk in, they see desks clustered together in groups of five or six. On each desk is a Post-it saying *M* or *F*. On the overhead is a direction, "Sit anywhere you like. Notice that *M* stands for male and *F* stands for female," letting students know that I value working together, across gender.

NAMING YOUR ROOM

Several years ago our school enrollment was so high that one class had to be moved from the building into a portable classroom. No one was eager to leave the building, but we generally agreed an older class would be more appropriate, since there would be no lavatory, no sink, no water. The portable classroom was placed in a corner of the playground, surrounded by unattractive blacktop. My class ended up there. It was pretty dismal at first, but the move became a lesson in making lemonade when you get lemons! We painted the door bright golden yellow and instead of being known as P–1, we named our classroom Paradise Island! It became a place where fantastic and wonderful things could happen. The students would love learning, and they would all succeed beyond their dreams. Ever since that year, my classrooms have had a name rather than a number. A decade later, I realize we set up a self-fulfilling prophecy. Naming our room created an overarching goal we tried to meet throughout the year.

DETERMINING CLASSROOM RULES

Organizational decisions are deeply rooted social studies activities. We've moved past that time when all the rules were in the teacher's head and students had to guess what they were through trial and error. Since the behaviorist movement, we've learned to clearly state and post our rules for expected behavior in the classroom. Now we are moving on to letting students determine their own rules.

I often start out in September by asking the class to brainstorm all the things we could do to make our classroom a terrible place, a place where no one would want to come, a place where we could guarantee no learning would occur.

As we list the surefire ways to kill a classroom, each suggestion more outrageous than the last, we begin to build a community. Eventually, when we have exhausted our efforts, most sincere and many hilarious, I ask the class to picture a room like the one we've just described. I ask them, What would you know if you stayed in a classroom like that one all year? What would you be able to do? How would you feel? After that discussion, it doesn't take long to reverse the list, identifying what needs to happen to make our classroom a place of joy where all students want to be and where all students can learn.

BUILDING A PEACEFUL CLASSROOM

In many ways, the classroom is a microcosm of the real world. There are the helpers and the hinderers, the care givers and the care takers, the lovable and the less lovable, just as there are in our neighborhoods, workplaces and business and social organizations. If there is something we value within groups, then we need to work toward it. I care about

Jon and Aaron find working and sharing together promotes peace and enriches learning.

peace. If I value peace in the world, then it seems to me I need to build peace in our classroom. So I begin conversations the first week of school about our classroom being a peaceful classroom (Drew 1987). We sit in a circle and describe the characteristics of peace.

"If you were describing peace, what words would you use?"

"I'd use the word calm."

"Calm is a great word. Close your eyes, everyone. Picture calm. What does calm look like?"

"It looks like a beautiful beach."

"I think it's gentle waves."

"It's a forest with no people in it."

"Calm is when I'm playing baseball really good."

"Calm is silence."

We build a shared understanding of peace. I make sure every child contributes, several times. Buy-in is so important at this early stage. If I can engage each child emotionally and intellectually in seeking peace, I know our classroom will support and encourage positive growth all year.

I talk to the students about why peace is important to me. I do my best to demonstrate how I make peace a reality in the classroom:

◆ I truly believe I can reach every child.
◆ I believe that catching children when they are good and acknowledging them is more powerful than punishment.

Chapter Two

- ◆ I have unconditional regard for each student.
- ◆ I believe learning is fun.

It begins with me!

PLANNING FOR PEACE

The students and I create an action plan for producing a peaceful classroom. This usually occurs the second week of school. This plan becomes our reference for classroom behavior, our "rule book." We have a discussion. We refer back to the first day when we listed all the things we could do to hinder learning. We recall the characteristics of peace. We talk about how some people like to work in a classroom that is noisy or has music playing and others need a quiet place. Discussion continues. It's not a quick process, but a vital one. The energy and time expended reaps all kinds of benefits later in the year in terms of classroom management. When we complete the action plan, each child signs it and so do I. (Figure 2–1 is an action plan created by a recent class.) I send a copy home. I want parents to understand what we value in our classroom. When misbehavior does occur, I then have a place to begin discussing my concern: You recall the action plan for peace the class created in September? I'm very concerned about Nancy because she doesn't seem to be able to help the class reach this goal. Specific things about Nancy's behavior that have prompted my concern are . . .

To turn these kinds of decisions over to students requires confidence and trust on the part of the teacher. I heard Horace Smith, formerly with the Seattle Public Schools, talk about this one day in a teacher training session in Renton, Washington. He pointed out how teachers with low self-esteem develop their classroom organization differently from teachers who have high self-esteem. I found his insights to be very helpful as a quick check of my own behavior.

Smith says teachers with low self-esteem are likely to be more critical of students. They will complain more frequently about disciplinary problems and lack of student motivation. You'll hear them using terms such as *obedience, laying down the law,* and *demanding respect.* They are the ones who often campaign for tougher school policies and more stringent punishments. They find it difficult to form friendly relationships with students for fear their authority will be undermined. These teachers tend to focus on student limitations rather than potential.

On the other hand, teachers with high self-esteem treat every child with unconditional regard. They encourage students to test their abilities

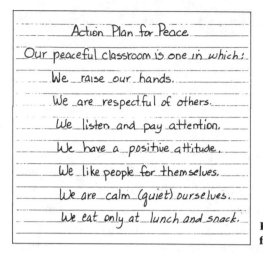

Figure 2–1: An action plan for peace.

and to set personal goals for themselves. They accept their students. These teachers help students develop problem-solving strategies. They build a sense of trust in their students by first modeling trust. Teachers with high self-esteem help students develop an internal locus of control, basing classroom control on understanding, joint cooperation, and working problems through.

Distinguishing between these two kinds of teachers altered my teaching behavior significantly. I always perceived myself as a teacher with high self-esteem. Yet, as I analyzed my behavior, I discovered that I did not treat all children with unconditional regard. Sometimes I blamed children for my lack of success. I occasionally thought, What's wrong with that kid? Why doesn't she try harder? Why doesn't he work more carefully? Why don't they act more pleasantly and do what I want them to do? I was trying to make students fit my convenience. I was not accepting them as they were. It seems so self-centered now. And it was.

Reflecting upon these observations snapped me from a no-win position. The simple words "unconditional regard for every child" freed me from the bondage of perceiving children as I wished them to be rather than as they are. I no longer get angry or aggravated with my students. My patience has increased tenfold. I enjoy every single day. I can laugh at my mistakes and help my students laugh at theirs. My classroom is no longer a contest of wills, it is a collaboration of willingness.

SHARING WISDOM AND HOPE

I read stories to the children. "Stories of wisdom and hope," my friend Barbara Inman calls them. These are stories that highlight universal truths like honesty, caring, and sharing; that reinforce common bonds; that promote prosocial behavior or resolve persistent dilemmas in positive ways. These stories make us dream, affirming our creativity and reminding us how worthwhile pursuing the impossible is. Examples include Chinese myths, Indian legends, African tales, Japanese folklore, or old fairy tales with a feminist twist, all of which have to do with valuing, maintaining perspective, and making choices. Using traditional cultural stories, especially those retold by authors indigenous to the culture, keeps me from reinforcing old stereotypes or inventing new ones as the students and I look for cultural connections. Understanding and respecting different points of view is a valued social studies skill.

Sometimes we discuss the story, sometimes we don't. When we do, it is to share feelings and to discover what we would have done in that situation. When we don't, it's because of something I learned from an American Indian storyteller. Northwest Coastal storytellers never analyze their stories with their listeners. They feel that every person who hears the story will take away what he or she heard. Sounds pretty obvious, doesn't it? I, however, talk everything to death. Maybe, just maybe, people hear what they hear because of where they are at the time. Maybe when they hear the story again, they'll hear something different. And maybe what they hear is exactly right for them at that time.

MEDIATING IN THE CLASSROOM

One thing for sure in fifth grade, there will be differences of opinion. We use mediation when the difference can't be easily addressed. In my classroom, the first week of school, we begin identifying problems that might need mediation. I ask the students to think back to problems they had that bothered them at school year before. After we've listed four or five of these on the board, the students get into groups to role-play the STAKE steps our school adopted three years ago to help students solve their own problems (see Figure 2–2). The STAKE steps are the result of six months of meetings with fourth and fifth graders to devise a mediation strategy for all the children in our school.

Setting Up for Success

Figure 2–2: Lakeridge students create a GEM (goodwill, equity, mediation) of a little book to teach mediation skills.

I begin by putting five students together and giving them a scenario of a typical playground problem, like arguing over a kick ball call or cutting someone out of a game. One student is identified as the mediator. A couple of students adopt one point of view, and the others take opposing perspectives. In front of the whole class, we begin the role-playing. As the problem unfolds, the mediator steps in. The conversation goes something like this:

Mediator: Hi, is there a problem?

Group: Yes.

Mediator: Would you like me to help you solve it?

Group: Sure.

Mediator: My name is Jerry. What's yours? (*Introductions go all around if the students don't know one another.*) Let's start with John. John, what do you think the problem is? (*Each child shares his or her point of view.*) Let's see if we can brainstorm some solutions. Who has an idea about how we might solve this? (*The involved students offer suggestions.*) Which one can you all accept? (*The group reaches a consensus.*)

My quietly coaching the students from the side seems to help prepare the students for successful problem solving. Working on the principle that those involved in the problem need to generate a solution removes authority (teacher, principal, whoever is bigger or tougher) from the matrix. Our students need to solve problems in a peaceful way themselves.

We also spend a lot of time talking about this quotation: "Mediation begins with Me." We explore its meaning and whose responsibility it is to solve problems. We make posters of children solving problems and create more role plays to remind ourselves when problems arise.

When the mediation process is firmly set for each student, I remove myself from playground squabbles, tattling, and issues of fairness. When I need to, I simply say, Would you like me to get you a mediator? Mediation makes classroom management easier.

In our school, the upper-grade students train the lower grades in the STAKE steps. Mediation is the option of choice for problem solving. The process of mediation is accessible to all the students in our school, K–5, because we believe that all students, not just a chosen few, need to master the skills of mediation. Therefore, fourth and fifth graders

41

become trainers for the primary grades. Once a year they go into every classroom in the school and present a program that includes role-playing, a panel discussion, and questions from the class. Two times a month, primary children are invited to have lunch with their intermediate-grade partners to discuss playground problems and mediation strategies and to play games that teach cooperation and compromise.

DECIDING JOBS

On one of the first days of school, we brainstorm the jobs that will need to be done each week. These usually include lunch monitors, attendance taker, messenger, classroom librarian, and "humor masters." This last job is one I recently added in my room. Each week two students share some humorous stories or jokes with the class. At first it seems like a silly job, an easy one. The students soon discover that choosing appropriate humor and pulling it off takes skill. I guide their initial choices, and we acknowledge all efforts in a thoughtful way. The students soon value the ability to tell a good story and make people laugh. It also lightens our classroom and makes it a fun place to be.

We choose the jobs by a lottery system. All the students' names are placed on cards and put in an old pencil box. Each Monday morning, we draw out cards until all the classroom jobs are filled. I note on each card what jobs each student has done so no one repeats a job until everyone has had a turn. This lottery system works well in my classroom for all kinds of choosing. The children think it's fair.

Acting Right

During the first week of school, the principal, the school counselor, and other people come to our classroom to explain their roles and how they want to assist the students during the year. I think these visits set the tone for how students behave when speakers come into the classroom or when we go to assemblies, so I teach the kids the four A's right away. I learned these from Julie Gustafson (1986), a children's drama teacher. They are:

Attend:	Listen to the presenter. Give your complete attention.
Allow:	Let the presenter share information.
Appreciate:	Acknowledge the talent, skill, information, risk, or time that the presenter is giving to you. It

takes time to prepare. It's a risk to stand up in
front of people to share anything.

Applaud: Express your appreciation through applause.

Over the past few years, I've noticed that many of my students have
forgotten how to clap. They hoot, whistle, stamp their feet, and wave
their fists, or they do nothing. The four A's reintroduces applause as an
acceptable way to express appreciation.

The four A's are also a guide to proper behavior when peers are
presenting in the classroom, which happens often. Valuing and supporting a peer's efforts are important in building everyone's confidence.
These, too, are social studies activities. Helping students become self-
disciplined and sensitive to others is important in becoming a good
neighbor and a good citizen.

Taking Temperatures
Another thing I do the first week is "take temperatures." At the close
of each day the students fill out cards with the following information:

One thing I did today.
One thing I learned today.
One thing I felt today.
One thing I'd change.

This information helps me to be sensitive to special needs and to see
how the students are reacting to what we are doing to build community,
self-esteem, and competence. Here are some sample responses:

One thing I learned was the 4 A's. I started my storyboard
and did some math. I felt good because people were nice to
me. Tomorrow I hope we do an art thing and do the humor
master.

I learned about the International Communication System. I
started my storyboard and practiced some math. I felt happy
because I'm starting to understand this school better.

Tomorrow I hope we have P.E. I learned the six elements of
a story. I played kick ball at recess and started my storyboard.
I felt sad because the day went by so quickly. Tomorrow I
hope we play another game.

I learned a lot, I mean "A LOT" about sign language. It's really cool. I made 3 new friends! If every day was like this I wouldn't even want summer to come. I would like to read more tomorrow.

There are other ways to get a quick sense of how the class is feeling or reacting. Some teachers I know ask kids to show an open hand if they are feeling positive about something, make a fist if negative. Some teachers use happy faces and sad faces. All of these techniques help us "read" our classroom temperature, monitoring and adjusting as needed.

INTRODUCING ME

We also make a book the first week of school. Called *All About Me*, it is based on a form adapted from a 1970s Seattle Public Schools multicultural curriculum kit (see Figure 2–3). The students fill in the blanks in pencil the first day of school. When they finish, they bring their paper up to my desk, and we go over it together. This immediately gives me something to talk about personally with every child and guarantees the activity will be successful for everyone. I begin collecting information about prior experiences from these forms, I also find out how the students present themselves on paper. After our session, the children go over their writing with a fine black felt-tip marker. I started using this technique—pencil first, felt pen second—a few years ago when we started publishing on a regular basis. I found that the children often took their edited papers back to their desks and in rewriting them made new mistakes! For quick publishing, this technique is hard to beat.

By Friday of the first week, we have published our first book. Out comes the lottery box. The student who "wins" gets to take the book home for the weekend. On Monday afternoon, we'll have a second drawing. That student gets *All About Me* for that night. Tuesday, we draw again. On it goes, until every child in the class has had the book at least one night. Every family has had an opportunity to see who else is in their child's classroom. This strategy helps build a sense of community, both within the classroom and in the homes of the students. (See page 165 in the appendix for a blank prototype of the form.)

IDENTIFYING YEARLONG THEMES

My overarching theme for the year is usually some variation of unity and diversity. This broadly stated theme is particularly appropriate be-

ME

NAME: _Peter_

HOME ADDRESS: _4836 84th Ave SE_

BIRTHDATE/AGE: _Oct 11 1982   10 yrs of age_

HOBBIES: _Stamps   Sports cards_

FAVORITE SPORT: _Football_

FAVORITE TV PROGRAM: _Rescue 911_

FAVORITE FOODS: _Mac + cheese_

FAVORITE BEVERAGE: _Coke   Dr. Pepper_

FAVORITE COLORS: _Orange_

FAVORITE SUBJECT: _Math_

FAVORITE SAYING: _What goes around comes around_

FAVORITE BOOK: _Hatchet by Gary Paulsen_

FAVORITE PLACE TO VISIT: _Library_

SOMETHING I'M PROUD I'VE DONE: _Finish 5th in the midlakes division for the 50 breaststroke_

FUTURE OCCUPATION: _Doctor_

Figure 2–3: *All About Me* is one of the first activities we do to build a classroom community.

Setting Up for Success

cause fifth graders and the fifth-grade curriculum are so diverse. Building a community of learners with a unity of purpose is paramount to having a successful year. Getting ready for middle school means fostering greater appreciation for differences and developing greater competence in working with others. Our fifth-grade social studies curriculum exemplifies unity and diversity through the study of U.S. history.

I like yearlong themes. They act as a central organizer for the choices I make. However, it is not a particularly overt theme for me. There is no major bulletin board dedicated to it, nor do I follow it rigidly. Instead, it is an "internal organizer." I share it with the class but I don't belabor it.

Picture books like Spier's *People* (1980) and Knight's *Talking Walls* (1992) are especially helpful in setting up an awareness of and an appreciation for diversity. We become "biphrasal" rather than bilingual, as students bring in greetings from other languages. We write each greeting on a large card and display it in the room. We use the phrases as we greet each other during the day. We learn a variety of sign language techniques the first two weeks of school. These are small activities, almost incidental, but ones in which awareness and appreciation for diversity are fostered, laying out the foundation for teaching tolerance and erasing prejudice. They are other examples of social studies happening all day in the classroom.

CONSTRUCTING THE BRAIN-COMPATIBLE CLASSROOM

Students should go home each night with a positive attitude. When the kids are happy, the parents are happy. When positive school talk is happening at home, positive behaviors happen at school. It is the beginning of a cycle of success that pays big dividends later in the year. Setting up the "brain-compatible classroom" (Kovalik 1993) right from the first day, adding humor, changing the pace of activities, and insisting that the action plan for peace be followed are ways that work with my students. Kovalik identifies eight components in the brain-compatible classroom, which I discuss below in the context of my classroom.

Absence of Threat
I accomplish this through our action plan for peace, by demonstrating unconditional regard for every student, and by making mistakes an "expectable" part of our learning process.

I encourage my students to make at least one mistake a day during the first month of school. Some children get so uptight at the beginning

46

of the year that they dig themselves a hole (of defeat, of self-criticism, of negativity, of poor work habits) and have a hard time coming out of it. When mistakes are made on purpose, they lose their power to embarrass or belittle. The children loosen up and they aren't so afraid.

Sometimes we take a "mistake break" at the end of the day, just so everyone has an opportunity to make one. The children and I talk about making mistakes. Risk taking means mistake making. We talk about the kinds of risks we can take in the classroom and the kinds of things we can learn from our mistakes. We identify how we can behave when we make mistakes and how we can support a peer who is mistaken. We begin to practice the art of informing people when they are wrong. Making mistakes becomes an expected part of learning and growing in our classroom.

Meaningful Content
The first day of school I try to teach my students at least one thing they've never known before that will last a lifetime. I use an international sign language the children can use in the classroom, when they travel, or when they meet people who don't speak English. Connecting learning to the students' prior knowledge and experience and projecting it into the future makes it meaningful.

Choices
Selecting what to read, determining how our room is organized, and deciding how to demonstrate competency are some of the choices my students have during the first month of school. They determine, for instance, how many independent reading books should be required and how the independent reading grade will be determined.

Adequate Time
I find this component much easier to accommodate because of our integrated curriculum. I don't have to stop the kids midstream in an activity just because it's time for social studies, or science, or art. Instead we can take the time to work in depth using blocks of time at our discretion.

Enriched Environment
Reading stories aloud, finding patterns, examining artifacts, filling the room with books, and providing visual interest through student-made murals are pieces of an enriched environment. Speakers from the community, videos that fit and extend the curriculum, field trips outside

the classroom, and movement within it are also part of enriching the environment.

Collaboration

Kovalik defines collaboration as students teaching each other and providing a sounding board for each other. In my classroom, students work together to achieve common goals, solving problems that matter. For example, early in the year my students create a mural of a Northwest forest as it was before the Europeans arrived . The project is integrated with our study of Northwest Coastal Indians and the classification of plants and animals. The kids identify animals that would have been plentiful in Northwest woods prior to 1840. They each research one animal and share their findings. In groups, they determine what plants would be indigenous. Working collaboratively, the students design and create a forest on our classroom wall. The children each contribute a three-dimensional model of the animal they researched. Each animal is appropriately placed in the mural, creating a scene that becomes "Our Northwest Woods."

Immediate Feedback

I quit correcting most daily work years ago. When the assignment is short, I figure students should correct their work themselves. In spelling,

A 1840s Northwest forest is created in our classroom by the Class of 2001.

the single biggest factor in increased performance is self-correction. If true in spelling, then it's probably equally true for other detail, practice-oriented learning activities, like daily math practice. If kids don't "see" their mistakes, they seldom quit making them. Most of the work in my room is long-term, comprehensive, and often project oriented. To help students succeed, we spend time talking about what an outstanding product looks like. As students progress with projects, I frequently hold up partially completed work and ask, What is particularly effective about this paper? What makes this look or sound so good?

Mastery

Most of the time, I ask the students to assess themselves. Often we develop rubrics before beginning the assignment. I want students to be able to identify particularly effective pieces of their work and to verbalize what they can do to improve. We use the notion of "personal best" in my classroom to get away from competitiveness.

Sometimes the students really want me to "grade" their work. They are interested in my opinion. I often choose to use symbols rather than numbers or letters. A plus means I think the work is outstanding. A check-plus means the work is quite wonderful but there are some inconsistencies. A check means I can live with it if the student can. A minus means the student is volunteering to do the assignment over. I prefer to use a rubric or a continuum to indicate where they are in the process (beginning, developing, capable, strong, exceptional). Frequently, I write a note to each student, relating improvements in this work to similar work in previous assignments.

Humor

Although Kovalik doesn't list this as a component of a brain-compatible classroom, I think humor and fun ought to be added. No one should grow without laughter.

REFLECTIONS

Intermediate-age students are quite self-centered in their point of view. Yet they are vulnerable, caring, and loving. They are also extremely concerned about fairness and equity. These seemingly contradictory attributes are the basis for building a successful school year for each child. I have learned it is my responsibility to build a teacher-student relationship based on trust. Helping students become more "other" directed and aware of multiple perspectives is one of my major goals.

Here's what I say to myself the first day of school and every day thereafter:

- Start with each child.
- Identify and recognize each child as a unique person who comes with experiences and knowledge.
- Provide that child with opportunities to make choices.
- Give each child as much control over the learning environment as possible.
- Surround each child with positive models of behavior that promote the common good.
- Support each child's independence with strategies to solve problems.
- Develop a community of learners as quickly as possible.
- Foster that sense of community by having unconditional regard for each child.
- Reach each child.
- Teach each child.

Chapter Three

IMPLEMENTING INTEGRATION

SOCIAL STUDIES TEACHING AND LEARNING
IS POWERFUL WHEN IT IS INTEGRATIVE.
—NCSS's *Vision*

CHANGING THE HIERARCHY

It seems as if a hierarchy of importance develops when we teach by subject. For instance, reading and math have driven the elementary-school day for years. As teachers adjusted their schedules to meet planned contingencies, such as assemblies and field trips, as well as unplanned emergencies, like snowstorms and power outages, they would think, I've got to get reading in first and then math. I can put off social studies until tomorrow. Today's teacher doesn't necessarily plan that way. When the day is integrated, the teacher might think, We'll continue reading our chapter book about the Inuit boy, make predictions in our reading journals, compile and classify data about Eskimo life, work in small groups to complete our mural of Arctic animals, and teach each other Eskimo counting games. Instead of feeling obligated to get in certain subjects at the expense of others, the teacher in an integrated classroom looks at the amount of time available as a whole rather than as pieces. Teacher and student stress is certainly reduced when one is not struggling to get in a subject fragment before the end of the day!

For me, the essential skills of social studies have been the primary means for integrating the curriculum. To apply and master these skills, a student needs to be able to "read, write, and do 'rithmetic." Rather than use subjects to order my day, I frequently connect data-gathering skills, intellectual skills, decision-making skills, and interpersonal skills across the curriculum. I use the term *block* to indicate to my students when we are working in an integrated fashion. Our local high school has a humanities/social studies core "block" class for advanced placement students. This class appeals to highly motivated and academically successful students. Because we live on an island, three miles by seven, everyone in the community knows about the block class. I decided if the high school could have a block, so could we.

ESSENTIAL SKILLS OF SOCIAL STUDIES

No matter the content that needs to be taught, certain skills fundamental to social studies education need to be developed. These are (NCSS 1990):

1. Data-gathering skills. Learning to:
   - Acquire information by observation.
   - Locate information from a variety of sources.
   - Compile, organize, and evaluate information.
   - Extract and interpret information.
   - Communicate orally and in writing.

2. Intellectual skills. Learning to:
   - Compare things, ideas, events, and situations on the basis of similarities and differences.
   - Classify or group items into categories.
   - Ask appropriate and searching questions.
   - Draw conclusions or inferences from evidence.
   - Arrive at general ideas.
   - Make sensible predictions from generalizations.

3. Decision-making skills. Learning to:
   - Consider alternative solutions.
   - Consider the consequences of each solution.
   - Make decisions and justify them in relationship to democratic principles.
   - Act based on those decisions.

4. Interpersonal skills. Learning to:
   - See things from the point of view of others.
   - Understand one's own beliefs, feelings, abilities, and shortcomings and how they affect relations with others.
   - Use group generalizations without stereotyping and arbitrarily classifying individuals.

- Work effectively with others as a group member.
- Give and receive constructive criticism.
- Accept responsibility and respect the rights and property of others.

STUDYING CULTURES

My belief that every child can learn needs to be made real to my students. Therefore, I start with an interesting focus for study, not where the social studies text begins. The text suggests spending several days introducing the elements of social studies in a very didactic format. My experience tells me to get into some wonderfully engaging knowledge and to discover the elements of social studies by doing. Weaving in an application of the essential skills while integrating our day and the content of our learning, I can make sure that every single child succeeds. One thing I've learned is to begin with fabulous, luscious, incredibly delightful information and to choose an initial activity all children can do—and do well. Making it open ended, giving plenty of latitude, and planning for diversity in both the approach and the outcome of the assignment invites every learner to succeed. Culture studies offer a wealth of interesting and intriguing information for all ages of students. I find culture studies an irresistible topic to engage students early in the year, and this is the blueprint I follow:

- Begin with a visual hook.
- Provide plenty of resources for information gathering.
- Develop a strategy for organizing data.
- Find literature to read aloud and read alone that reveals different points of view.
- Give an opportunity to compare or classify attributes on the basis of similarities and differences.
- Examine artifacts, bring in resource people, and/or go on field trips.
- Experience the culture through art, music, dance, and stories.
- Create a culminating activity to synthesize learning.
- Encourage student reflection (What did I learn? What did I do? How do I feel?)

The remainder of this chapter discusses two culture studies I've used.

"ARCTIC ADVENTURE: AWARENESS AND APPRECIATION"

Presenting the Visual Hook

Today I'm going to start with a short film, *Across Continents*, on Inuit (Eskimo) people as an introduction to our First Peoples focus. I've found children tend to learn visually first. If I give them a visual image when I introduce a new focus of study, I am giving them a common storehouse of knowledge from which to draw. I usually use a picture book, but this particular film shows the connections between Siberian people and Alaskan indigenous groups. One of my objectives is for the students to be aware of the land bridge theory as we look at the inhabitation of the Americas. My main goal is for the students to realize that there are many different groups of Inuit people, each having unique customs and traditions but whose culture has been shaped by the environment of the Far North. This goal also demonstrates the concept of unity and diversity. Before showing the film, I give the students five minutes to list everything they know about Inuit people. The stereotype of Nanook of the North runs deep, I see, as the students share the knowledge that all Eskimos live in igloos and ask, What's an Inuit?

Preparing Data Disks

After the film, I ask the students, "Is there anything you'd like to cross out on your list that you thought you knew but you've changed your mind about?" As the children revise their lists in small groups, I pass out a brief summary of the food, shelter, clothing, and language of fifteen different Inuit groups. The children learn that Arctic people in America called themselves Inuit, meaning "people." Eskimo was a name given them by the Abnaki Indians, meaning "eaters of raw meat" (Spizzirri 1989). Working in pairs, the students enter the information onto a "data disk" (see Figure 3–1). The data disk, round rather than rectangular, has proven to be an engaging way for intermediate-age students to gather data. Since the students are extrapolating existing data, everyone can accomplish this activity quickly and successfully.

When the data disks are complete, the students read a short informational article on the land bridge theory. Then each pair introduces their Inuit group to the class, sharing the information they collected. I record the data on an overhead chart as the students share. Pretty soon, we have a graphic display of data for comparing similarities and finding differences. We can hypothesize why some groups have developed differences and can form questions to be investigated.

Next, we begin to discuss the land bridge theory. I ask the students

Figure 3–1: Rachael's data disk shares basic information about one Inuit group.

to compare it to the legend I read to them after recess about how Inuit people came to Alaska. During the discussion, one child comments on how it seems that all cultures have creation stories. Since we will study several cultures this year, we decide to test this generalization, Do all cultures have creation stories? This generalization is the first of many threads that will weave our learning into a single cohesive piece throughout the year.

I share examples of Inuit art with the class. It usually intrigues the students because it is so unpredictable and seems humorous to them. We talk about the difficulty of living in such a harsh environment, using the atlas to verify our assumptions about climate and seasons.

We hypothesize about the kinds of clothing, hats, and weapons used. Tomorrow will be a field trip to a local museum that has an Inuit display. We discuss things to look for and review the questions they raised earlier. Perhaps we can find the answers tomorrow. It's lunch already!

Building a Cohesive Classroom

After lunch is reading workshop. This sixty-five-minute period is devoted to reading and reading-related activities. Sometimes the children read anything they choose. Sometimes they read material I assign them. Today, we begin reading *Eskimo Boy*, by Pipaluk Freuchen (1951). The central character in this vivid story of survival and courage is an Inuit boy in Greenland. The preface has a pronunciation page to help the children with the unusual Eskimo names—a perfect time for a quick pronunciation-key minilesson. After about ten minutes of review and practice using the key to pronounce names, I begin reading the story aloud while the students either follow along or just listen. Getting the children into the rhythm of the story, answering their initial questions, and setting them up for success are important, particularly early in the year and especially when the story is required reading.

How much or how often I should dictate the reading material of my students is a question I ask continually. It's another balancing act. I want the students to have some shared knowledge so our discussions can be inclusive. I've come to realize that reading the same material provides exactly the kind of community-based knowledge one strives for in today's classroom. No one is excluded from the common ground. In the integrated classroom, knowledge is the root of all the activities. Manipulating what is known—recalling it, analyzing it, putting it together in new forms, wondering about it, and making decisions about it—is what happens. Common knowledge is a club that everyone belongs to. Nobody is left out when we read the same story, discuss the same dilemmas, and evaluate decisions together.

Building Equity in the Classroom

Reading the same information also has to do with equity. All children have the right to have access to the same information. In a truly social studies–integrated classroom, equity is the cornerstone of the democratic ideal. All children should have access to the same level of knowledge. That's why grouping is cooperative, fluid, and often self-selected. Reading the same story acts as a common catalyst for our classroom. The story or article is often the springboard for examining issues, extending knowledge, and enriching appreciation. (See Chapter 7 for a detailed discussion about the issues of equity in the classroom.)

Getting into the Story

Back to *Eskimo Boy*. I read the first chapter aloud and then ask the students to write down at least one question they hope to answer by the time they finish the book and to write down at least one prediction. When they have finished, they share their questions and their predictions. Now comes silent reading time. Early in the year, ten minutes is about as long as they can sustain the reading. Later, many can read thirty minutes at a "sit," though some still fade after ten minutes.

Taking out their literature response journals, the students write for about fifteen minutes. Perhaps they will identify words, phrases, or paragraphs they find memorable. For this type of entry I have them use a double-entry format that I learned from Patricia Hagerty. I find it encourages thoughtful exploration. The students draw a line down the center of their notebook page. On the left-hand side they list interesting words, phrases, or whole paragraphs from the book. Adjacent, on the right-hand side, they tell why they chose to record these particular words, phrases, or paragraphs. (Figure 3–2 shows some examples by Alyssa and Julie, experienced double-entry journal writers.)

The students have other options for their journal responses. They may choose to write about what they know so far or how they feel. I try to open the door to all learning styles. They may write a poem about Ivik, the Eskimo boy, or they may write him a letter. What they choose to write in their journals is essentially their own decision. But write they must. Over the year, I model additional forms of written communication and work with individual students to set goals that will enhance and extend their knowledge and skill.

After about fifteen minutes, I ask the students if anyone would like to share what has been written. Several children usually do. I do this daily if I can, because I think it validates the writing, stimulates other students' thinking, and lets me know what's going on. I read the journals once a week—seven a day for four days—and talk to the students once a week about their writing. I like this workshop approach because it facilitates the success of all readers in my classroom, regardless of ability. It promotes learning and prompts critical thinking by the reader as a writer and as a listener. I especially enjoy the autonomy it gives me. It's great not to have to lug a huge reading manual around anymore! The workshop format of read, respond, and share makes learning much

<u>Double-Diary Entry</u>

Words, Phrases, and Paragraphs	Why I chose to record these
Maryark does not scream; strangely enough, he looks as though he was. Ivik knows that his look must be from pain. Then Maryark's face disappears. That is the last Ivik sees of his father.	I thought that paragraph was loaded with melancholy. I watched Maryark along with Ivik helplessly as he vanished under the water. For a vivid moment I thought he would survive. I was wrong
"Oh, no" says Otonia, Ivik's brother. "My big brother's kayak is so used to going out hunting that now it goes alone."	That was a funny thought. He was so little he didn't know the difference.
On a still summer day in Greenland, when the arctic sea is as smooth as oil would have been.	This makes me want to go and feel oil to see how smooth the sea was.

Figure 3–2: Excerpts from Julie's and Alyssa's double-entry diary

more natural now. It flows. By supporting, connecting, and extending knowledge in reading and social studies, integration fosters a tapestry of learning, making the whole day significant.

Gathering Information

After the last recess, we begin a short, integrated language arts project. Many new vocabulary words and concepts are revealed as we learn about the Arctic and the Arctic people. I want to know what is "sticking" and what is not. I also want to discover what skills the students are using comfortably this early in the year. This strategy lets me observe learning orientation. Does the child tend to use words or pictures to communicate? Does he choose to work independently or does he gravitate toward groups? Does she take intellectual risks or does she play it safe with known information, familiar facts? Conversations about Inuits and Arctic life are spontaneous. I listen for understanding and misunderstanding.

An ABC organizer seems to be a perfect project for revealing this information and is an activity that will be successful for every child (See page 166 in the appendix for detailed plans). We scour the library for resources: picture books, reference works, fiction, and nonfiction. After dividing a large sheet of white paper into squares, the students prepare an Arctic ABC chart. Using any of the resources, they begin finding words/ideas/concepts that are a part of the Arctic or Inuit life to place on the chart. Our challenge is to find at least one word for each letter of the alphabet. Some of the children, noticing the books of Inuit/Eskimo legends placed around the room, begin perusing them. Others get out their copy of *Eskimo Boy*. Others look back at the data disks. A couple of kids go to the encyclopedia, while one girl heads for the computer, which has *Compton's Encyclopedia* on disk. It's a scavenger hunt. Fun, but focused. And the day ends, too quickly. We have lots to do tomorrow!

Using Topical Math

Math begins this new day. It's a short period, since we have the field trip. We start with a mental math exercise, adding columns of numbers. To make it more relevant, I present the problems in terms of the hunters from a Yupik village that have been working on their stores for the winter. In the storehouse, Ivik counts the following: 16 otters, 8 caribou, 32 seals, and 10 musk-ox. How much does the village have in all? A second village has been hard at work too. They have 9 snow geese, 1 moose, 15 rabbits, 20 salmon and 1 whale. Which village has the most food? The fun part of this is the discussion about whether the largest quantity really indicates the most food. Is a whale worth 32 seals? Good questions. It lets me see into how the children think. It helps them understand written story problems. Tying computational math to the current topic makes it relevant and fun. Connecting conceptual math to the theme creates another way of knowing.

Taking a Field Trip

Its time to get ready for the field trip. We begin with a quick reminder of appropriate field trip behavior, slightly modifying the four As:

- ◆ Allow the guides to tell you what they know. They may answer one of your questions.
- ◆ Appreciate that most guides are volunteers and give freely of their time and talents to help us know more.
- ◆ Pay attention to what is going on around you. Look at the displays, notice details. Be aware. When the group moves, move with it. Be sensitive to the needs of others in the museum by keeping your voice down and walking quietly.
- ◆ Applaud your guide at the end of the tour to express your appreciation. And don't forget to have fun!

Quickly, I show the students how to fold a piece of paper into a little book for taking notes (see Figure 3–3). A whole language strategy I learned from a primary teacher, I use the little book constantly in my classroom. (See page 167 in the appendix for extensions.) Ubiquitous, versatile, and ecological, little books fit into every unit of study. They help organize observations for later reference and reflection. (Thank you, whoever created the little book format! You've given a wonderful gift to teachers and students.)

The field trip proves worthwhile. The students see many examples of the ways the environment shaped the culture of various Inuit groups. They marvel over the resourcefulness of the people of the North and are fascinated by their creativity. Many find answers to questions they have formed. Several discover facts to add to the Arctic ABC chart. Their little books focus mostly on sketching artifacts and listing materials the Inuits used to survive in Arctic conditions.

Putting Out a Newspaper in a Day

We list everything we can remember on the board when we return from the field trip. Then we have a lottery. The first child whose name

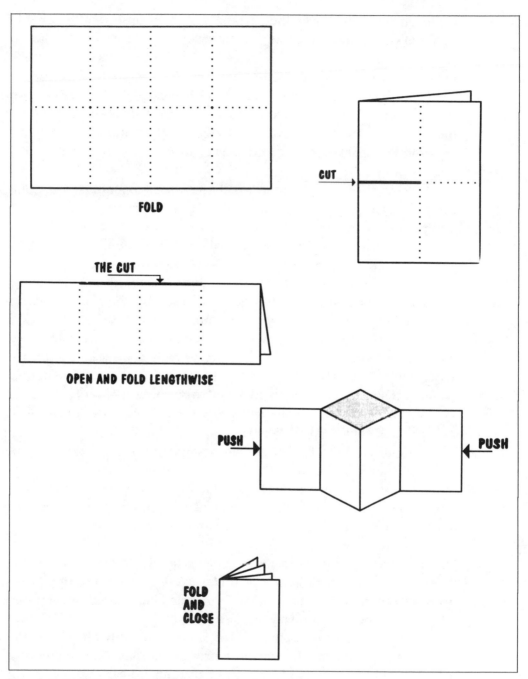

FOLD

CUT

THE CUT

OPEN AND FOLD LENGTHWISE

PUSH **PUSH**

FOLD AND CLOSE

Figure 3–3: Little books work magic as an integrative strategy.

is picked from the "lucky lottery box" gets to choose what he or she wants to write about from this list. The second child gets second choice and so on, until every child has selected one of the items on the board to write about. Since this is our first writing assignment, I decide to use it as baseline data about each child's writing skill. A newspaper is an appropriate medium, since we have news to share about our trip to the museum. It's also a good way to share information with parents regarding the field trip. We need to take advantage of our community resources by moving our learning beyond classroom walls.

Newspapers in a day! The way real newspapers operate, not the old three-weeks-to-get-it-all-together kind of newspaper we used to do. I quit doing newspapers for about a decade because they were so boring and so out of date by the time we finally finished them. Today's copy-machine technology makes all the difference in the world.

By drawing on observations made during the field trip and by tapping the accumulated store of knowledge acquired by the class's reading and research, each student can successfully contribute. Over the years, I've come to understand that we don't need to ask intermediate-grade students to write "long." We get more growth if we ask to students write "often." I've also noticed that if the shape of a piece of notebook paper is changed, the students often find the writing task more engaging. For this activity, the students are each given a "column"—a half sheet of notebook paper, cut vertically.

In about an hour, the articles are complete. I encourage students who finish early to illustrate their work. Then we edit the articles, and the students go over the final copy in black felt-tip pen. Total time: about an hour and a half of class time and an additional hour of teacher time spent reducing the columns, taping the mock-up together, and running the copies.

The newspaper looks terrific (a page is shown in Figure 3–4). We have proof of the value of our field trip. We have an interesting piece to read as a class tomorrow, a piece that demonstrates how well our class can work cooperatively and productively.

I can also use it for evaluation. The students identify their strengths and comment on what they might improve next time. The editing process points to what needs to be emphasized next. I can also see where content knowledge has been misunderstood and plan for clarification.

Using Picture Books and Stories to Teach Traditional Cultures
A new day. The students continue working on their Arctic ABC charts as they read books from the library about Inuits and their environment.

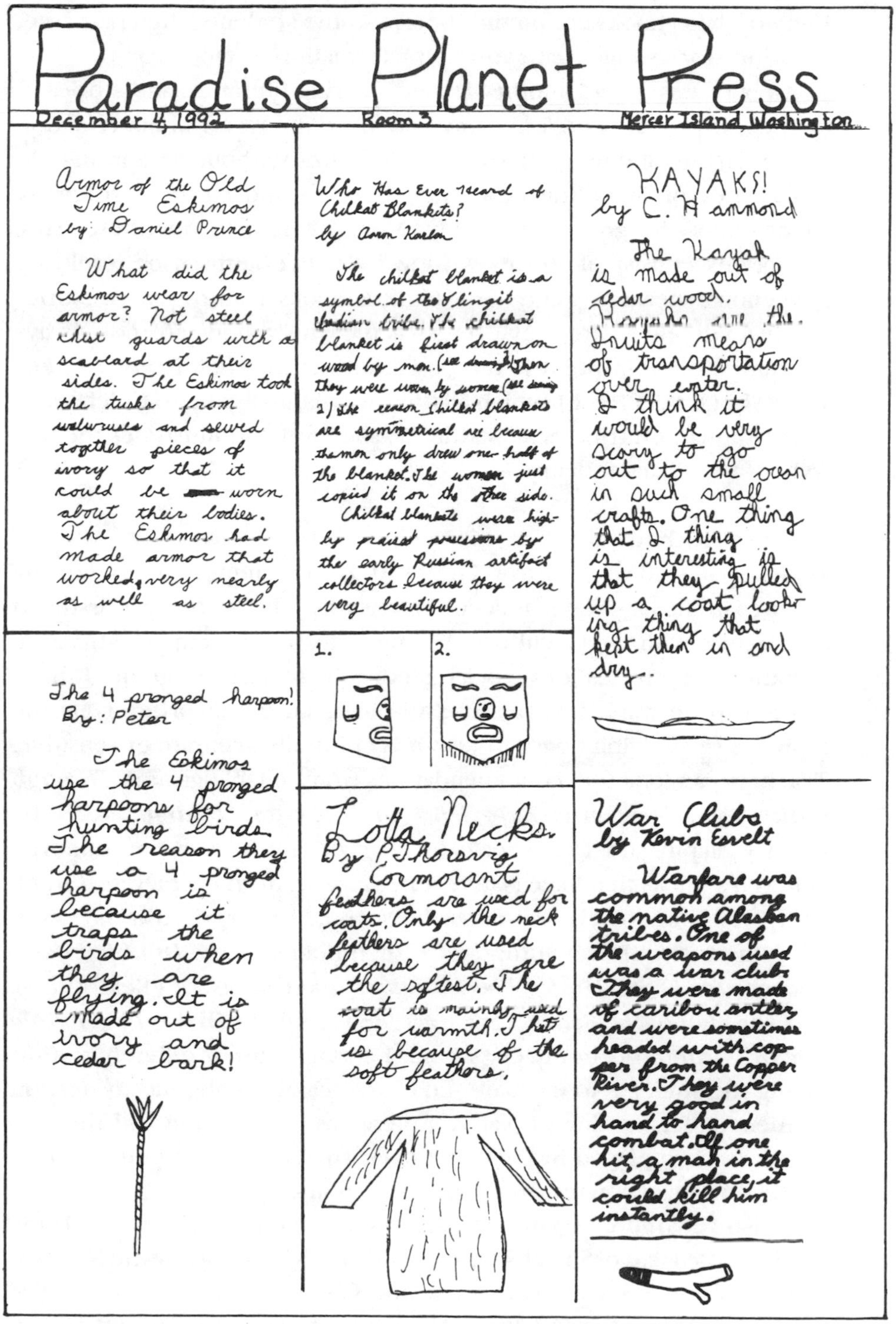

Paradise Planet Press

December 4, 1992 — Room 3 — Mercey Island, Washington

Armor of the Old Time Eskimos
by Daniel Prince

What did the Eskimos wear for armor? Not steel chest guards with a scabbard at their sides. The Eskimos took the tusks from walruses and sewed together pieces of ivory so that it could be ~~worn~~ worn about their bodies. The Eskimos had made armor that worked very nearly as well as steel.

Who Has Ever Heard of Chilkat Blankets?
by Aaron Karlin

The chilkat blanket is a symbol of the Tlingit Indian tribe. The chilkat blanket is first drawn on wood by men. (see drawing) Then they were woven by women (see drawing 2) The reason Chilkat blankets are symmetrical is because the men only drew one half of the blanket. The women just copied it on the other side.

Chilkat blankets were highly praised possessions by the early Russian artifact collectors because they were very beautiful.

KAYAKS!
by C. Hammond

The Kayak is made out of cedar wood. Kayaks are the Inuits means of transportation over water. I think it would be very scary to go out to the ocean in such small crafts. One thing that I thing is interesting is that they pulled up a coat looking thing that kept them in and dry.

The 4 pronged harpoon!
By: Peter

The Eskimos use the 4 pronged harpoons for hunting birds. The reason they use a 4 pronged harpoon is because it traps the birds when they are flying. It is made out of ivory and cedar bark!

1.   2.

Lotta Necks
By P. Thoreson

Cormorant feathers are used for coats. Only the neck feathers are used because they are the softest. The coat is mainly used for warmth. That is because of the soft feathers.

War Clubs
by Kevin Esvelt

Warfare was common among the native Alaskan tribes. One of the weapons used was a war club. They were made of caribou antler, and were sometimes headed with copper from the Copper River. They were very good in hand to hand combat. If one hit a man in the right place, it could kill him instantly.

Figure 3–4: Thanks to a classroom full of reporters, we have a newspaper in a day!

Implementing Integration

Many of these books are picture books, so the students often pair-read, enjoying stories together, gathering information in tandem.

After recess, I read another legend. Sharing literature and stories of the people we are studying is my way of trying to instill appreciation for similarities and differences among cultures without reinforcing old stereotypes or inventing new ones. I try to find stories written by members of the groups we study. More often than not these days, collections consist of stories written by native authors or retold by indigenous speakers. Many new picture books feature native stories and legends. Be aware, however, that the illustrations are not always accurate. A case in point is the powerful picture book *Brother Eagle, Sister Sky* (Jeffers 1991), which features words attributed to Chief Sealth of the Suquamish tribe near Seattle, Washington, but illustrates the life-style of the Plains Indians.

Seeking Authenticity

As a social studies educator I think it is very important to portray cultures in the classroom as accurately as possible. No one has firsthand experience with every culture. We need to rely on experts. Because literature permeates our social studies–centered program, I have learned to be wary. Just because a book is an old favorite or fits the topic we're studying doesn't mean it is culturally accurate or sensitive. Teachers can look for recommendations from reliable groups. *Through Indian Eyes: The Native Experience in Books for Children*, edited by Beverly Slapin and Doris Seale (1992), critiques over one hundred children's books that have Native Americans as main characters. I think many well-meaning classroom teachers would be surprised at the evaluation these two Indian authors give such books as *The Double Life of Pocahontas* (Fritz 1983), *The Indian in the Cupboard* (Reid 1980), and *The Sign of the Beaver* (Speare 1983). While I still use *The Double Life of Pocahontas* in my classroom, I certainly use it differently now, asking the students to evaluate the character of Pocahontas in relation to their understanding of Native Americans at that time and the role Indian women played in their particular society, pointing out discrepancies and inaccuracies from a different point of view.

I also rely more heavily on lists, such as Notable Children's Trade Books in the Field of Social Studies, which is a joint effort by the National Council for the Social Studies and the Children's Book Council. The readers who prepare this list represent many cultures, and ethnic authors are encouraged to submit their publications for consideration. A primary focus of this group is to identify literature that emphasizes human relationships, represents a diversity of groups, and is sensitive to a broad range of cultural experiences. This list, and a similar one on science, is available annually for free. Simply send a stamped, self-addressed six-by-nine-inch envelope to Children's Book Council, 568 Broadway, Suite 404, New York, NY 10012.

Using Picture Books and Stories to Teach Contemporary Cultures

Too often we leave cultures on the museum shelf, rather like the Indian in *The Indian In the Cupboard*. In the story, a young boy finds a magical cupboard that brings to life a miniature of an Indian. So too, classroom studies often focus on the exotic and the unusual of a culture, the old or the archaic. I think we have an obligation to share with our students the authentic life of native people today. Members of dynamic and vibrant cultures, they are a part of today's world. It doesn't matter whether we are studying American Indians, African Americans, or Chinese immigrants. Each culture needs to be studied in a contemporary context, not treated as an artifact to be taken out, examined, and put away again, folded within the pages of history. Picture books provide vivid and contemporary glimpses of life today in many cultures. So often, the cultures in these kind of resources are revealed through the eyes of children, as in *Eskimo Boy: Life in an Inupiaq Eskimo Village* (Kendall 1992). Let the school librarian know what cultures your class will be studying and emphasize that contemporary life will also be apart of that study.

Searching for Student-Centered Spelling

Reading, responding in the journal, and sharing continue in the afternoon. Time for a spelling pretest. Words are garnered from the newspaper editing, the journals, and the Arctic ABC chart, which have been our focus for this week. We average a basic list of about twenty words a week pertaining to what we are studying, or will be studying, as well as the most frequently misspelled words from student writing.

I'm not satisfied with our spelling integration. The once-a-week test seems to have little to do with increasing spelling competency. Studying isolated words has little impact on how one spells when one is writing. Perhaps its more important to know what words one can't spell—and to be able to find out how. I plan to work on helping kids spell better for their own benefit so they are more facile writers, more interesting wordsmiths and more conceptually capable of communicating on pa-

65

per. My own attempt at integrating spelling really has more to do with not isolating it as a separate subject but encouraging students to become aware of the words they use and how these words are put together. Spelling in our room emerges through language arts activities, often in a social studies context.

Introducing Points of View

During block, the students watch a Cousteau video of an Eskimo village. The thrust of the film is how compatible the life is with the environment and how it is changing as technology and contemporary life become more and more a part of the culture. I read to the students the book *In Two Worlds: A Yup'ik Eskimo Family*, by Aylette Jenness and Alice Rivers (1989), to give them yet another point of view. We discuss how Inuit life appears to have changed in our contemporary world. Has our life changed as well? The children decide to interview their parents or grandparents to find out what changes technology has made in their lives.

Working in groups of four, the students eagerly compare their lists of changes with one another, looking for similarities. Eliminating repetitions, they compile a new list. Then each group shares with the whole class. Obviously, technology is a powerful agent for change, regardless of the culture. We discuss the costs and benefits of technology in society. The discourse is thoughtful, energetic, and spontaneous. No conclusions are drawn, but I ask the students to tuck this conversation into their memory banks, since we'll revisit the effect of technology on cultures throughout the year. We've identified another thread in our integrated curriculum.

The Arctic ABC charts are nearly finished. Many are hanging around the room (see the example in Figure 3–5). Students enjoy looking at one another's work. I'm continually amazed by the diversity such a rudimentary assignment generates. In our evaluation session, the students decide that when they do an assignment like this again they'll make some presentation improvements—outlining the squares, writing more legibly, and illustrating as well as listing words.

Replicating Inuit Art

Copies of illustrations from legends and folktales depicting Inuit life in more traditional times that are displayed around the room call attention to the wildlife, the activities of the people, and the lines of the landscape. I show the class a block print of Inuit life done by a former student

Figure 3–5: Alexa collects Arctic words on her ABC chart.

Implementing Integration

using tagboard and printer's ink, and I then demonstrate how to make a similar print.

Having the copied illustrations available keeps the students more focused on the goal, which is to replicate Inuit art: a certain discipline is imposed. In many cultures, artists learn by copying: they are required to reproduce traditional form, line, and color. This is good practice for my students as well. Those who are insecure feel free to trace various shapes directly from the models. Others re-create the art through observation. Once children have tried to reproduce, authentically, the art of another culture, most of them internalize a respect and regard for that culture.

Reading to Learn

"Reading to learn" is an important skill to master in fifth grade, as is reading in a wide variety of genres. Reading short chapters rather than whole books decreases the fear of failing that some children have. Now that the students have a sense of and a connection with the people who live in the North, it's time to integrate earth science. Using an existing curriculum, I select particular chapters as the foundation of

Lindsey brings Inuit images to life through block printing.

Brad enjoys the printing process.

our study. This will to be reading-based study because it is important that students become capable readers for information. Much of what we will do the rest of the year is predicated on the ability to learn from reading. Extracting and interpreting information should be modeled by both the teacher and by peers. It should be practiced and mastered by each student.

Our next few days are divided between working on the block prints and reading and learning about land formations on earth. We talk about the importance of reading the questions first, so we know what to look for. We discuss why the editors draw pictures or graphs, what a bold-faced phrase or italicized word might signify to the reader. We practice reading fast and reading slow—changing our speed depending on the purpose.

I *don't* have them read the material and wait for me to tell them what they need to know, something I found myself doing in the past. Pretty soon, the clever kids figure out they don't need to read the chapter, they can just wait for me to tell them what they need to know. Now, as we begin to discover the process of reading to learn, I ask the students, what was one thing you learned from this reading? What was

Jill shares her final print.

something you had confirmed—something you thought you knew and, by golly, according to this reading, you did? What is something you are still confused or puzzled about? If you had to describe a moraine to a second grader, how would you do it? I don't answer the questions, they do. Back into the reading we go, to verify hypotheses and to confirm student responses.

Making the Community Connection

A parent comes in to share her collection of Inuit clothing and artifacts. She and her husband lived in an Inuit village several years ago. She shares some of her thoughts and observations about how she saw technology influencing Inuit lifestyles. She even brings her new husky puppy so the students can see a real sled dog. Sending thank you cards to her provides a real-life reason for writing.

Culminating the Story

Everyone has finished reading *Eskimo Boy*. Early in the reading, the students wrote letters as if they were Ivik, the Eskimo boy, describing his family's situation on the island. Now they write letters as if they were Ivik at the end of his adventure reflecting on what happened. The block prints are done. They write poetry to share their feelings and knowledge about the Arctic and Arctic life (see Figure 3–6).

The final activity is a short story, *Call It Courage* (Sperry 1940), about a boy's survival and courage in a South Pacific setting. Some years I read it aloud to the class. Some years each student reads an individual copy. Some years I show the video. After the story, the students compare the Inuit boy Ivik's situation with the South Pacific islander Mafatu's. The students sort similarities and differences. They identify a common theme of courage. Sharing comparisons in a class discussion leads to inferences and conclusions:

- ◆ "Courage is challenged by the environment."
- ◆ "Courage is from the inside out."
- ◆ "Anyone could be full of courage."
- ◆ "Any environment can become a matter of survival."
- ◆ "Good luck and good thinking make survival possible."
- ◆ "Anybody can have hard times."

The students know that we are going to move on to another culture, and they are reluctant to leave their friends, the Inuits. I hope this interest in studying cultures becomes lifelong.

70

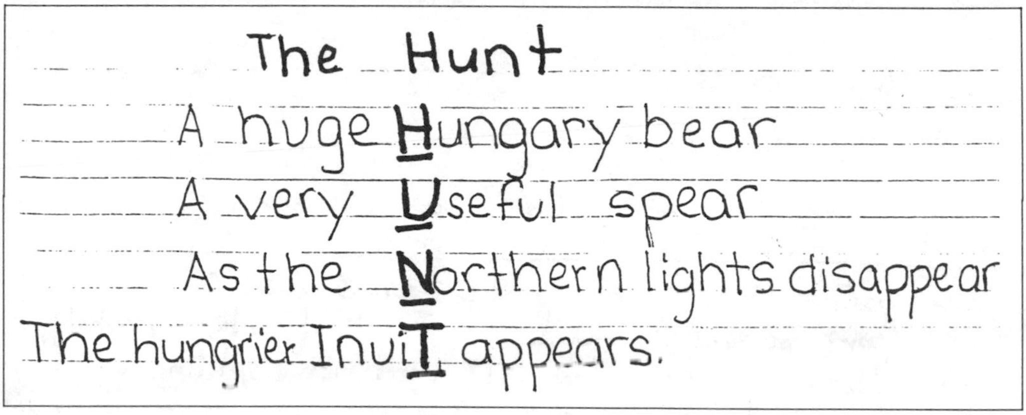

The Hunt

A huge **H**ungary bear
A very **U**seful spear
As the **N**orthern lights disappear
The hungrier Inui**T** appears.

Figure 3–6: David writes an acrostic poem.

"PEOPLE OF THE NORTHWEST COAST: PAST AND PRESENT"

Introducing Artifacts

A large wooden crate dominates the table in the back of the room. As the children enter, they poke it and question each other about the contents. I observe their interest but start the day out routinely. By midday, many have forgotten the crate's existence.

"Who knows what an anthropologist does?" Many guesses. Some close, some far afield, one right on! "Today, you are going to be anthropologists. In the box are artifacts from another culture. Each of you will draw an artifact and then develop a hypothesis about how it is used. Let's plan how you might do your work."

By drawing the artifact, the students will observe it carefully, look at the colors, feel the textures. In speculating about its use they will call on their prior knowledge and make assumptions about the culture the object came from. We practice making some hypotheses and assumptions about common articles around our classroom (the chalkboard eraser, the clock, the overhead). When the assignment seems clear, the box is opened. The artifacts are objects on loan from a local natural history museum specializing in Northwest Coastal Indian groups. Each child gets one artifact to examine. It's a quiet room now. Energy is concentrated on the artifacts. As the students finish, they hang their Artifact Find sheet (see Figure 3–7) on the bulletin board and place their artifact on the display table sitting beneath the bulletin board.

Curator's Name __Sara__

Artifact Find

Description:

part of it is wood. the blade is about 8 inches the rope that holds the blade on it it is probably leather, the rope is about half of a mm.

Possible Uses:

I think it is probably used for spliting wood. Or sneeking up on something and stab it.

Assumptions & Observations:

the people who made this are probably very smart and intellagent It probably took a long time to make.

Detailed Drawing:

Figure 3–7: Sara's Artifact Find sheet.

Relating Reading

During snack and story time, I begin reading legends dealing with Raven, a very powerful figure in Northwest Coast lore. A trickster, a changer, often a troublemaker, Raven is mirrored in many cultures. Coyote, Anansi, Brer Rabbit, and Monkey all play similar roles in Southwest Indian, African, African American, and Chinese folklore. Trickster tales are another cultural thread we will follow throughout the year.

The students begin reading the resource book *Indians of the Northwest Coast* (Garrod 1980). It will be our textbook for the next few weeks. Written as a narrative, short and child centered, the book is interesting and nonthreatening. Beginning with the geography and geology of the Northwest Coastal people, we review some of our earth science knowledge and add information about the coastal climate. We have no single piece of literature featuring Northwest Coastal people. Instead, I provide a list of potential read-alone books featuring American Indians from many different nations. "Here is a list of books that have American Indians as main characters. In the next three weeks, read at least two of them. Respond to them in your journal. Be ready to share your observations."

Then I do a book talk about each one. There are enough copies so that each child may choose a title right away, even though it might not be a first choice. Because several of the students are reading the same book, we will have group sharing sessions this week. That way, each group has an opportunity to discuss what it is reading and ask questions. In addition to those read-alone books, there are also several reference books about American Indians available around the room.

The next day, I become the guide and take the students on a "tour" of the artifacts. After we discuss each object, describe its use, and point out unusual or common characteristics, students reclaim their objects and fill out an Artifact Fact sheet (see Figure 3–8). Hanging the Facts sheet over the Find sheet, we discuss how anthropologists might make errors. We also observe how they can be incredibly accurate. *Motel of the Mysteries* (1979), a humorous book by David Macaulay that explores a motel as if it were a building from the distant past, becomes a favorite read-alone.

Teaching Peers, Reaching Across Ages

The students now prepare to become guides themselves. First, we decide to invite their kindergarten buddies and the third graders. They'll be our practice groups. Younger students are easier than peers, less

Curator's Name **Sara**

Artifact's Name **Elbow Adz**

Artifact Facts

Description: This elbow Adze has a metal blade tied on to a cedar handle with cedar strips. It is called an Elbow Adze because of its shape. We also know that it was made after European contact.

Use: This Adze is used for stripping bark off of a tree. It is also used for carving totempoles, shaping canoes and making planks for making houses.

Comments about the culture: The culture this Adze came from was very smart. In order to cut down a tree, they asked for its permission. They appreciated their environment and took care of it.

Detailed Drawing:

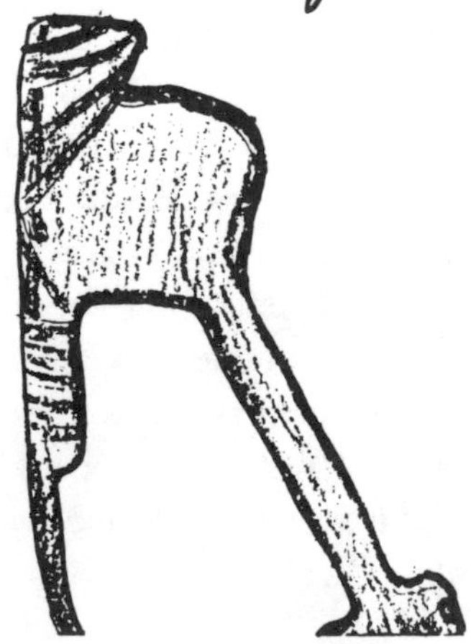

Figure 3–8: Sara's Artifact Facts sheet shows she has moved from "maybe" to "knowing."

intimidating. After that, we'll invite the other fifth-grade classes, since they study Northwest Coastal people too.

Practicing speaking clearly and loudly enough to be heard, keeping the presentation coherent and informational, maintaining poise and eye contact, each student gives his or her piece eight times. Those listening practice being good and supportive listeners. By the eighth round, each child in Paradise Island knows each artifact, how it's used, and its special characteristics. When asked to identify each artifact on a paper-and-pencil test, there's no problem. They can describe the artifacts' functions and tell why they had value to the people of that time and place. Everyone earns 100%. Fifth graders should practice taking tests, and they should be successful in their practice. I don't want to teach test phobias or practice test failures.

After the test, we discuss why they do so well. One student observes that they had "done" it eight times. Their conclusion? If a person really wants to know something, teach it the right way eight times! We do remember most of what we teach others. It's not a bad rule to figure out if you're a student, and it's great strategy to use if you're a teacher.

Teaching Your Passion

Teaching about Northwest Coastal people is one of my passions. I've taken classes, gone on trips, and read voraciously to deepen my keen interest in these diverse and talented people of the Northwest Coast. It's not so surprising, then, that I cheat just a little and stay with the Northwest topic just a little bit longer than planned each year. There is such a wealth of information. Northwest Coastal art, in particular, seems to strike a chord with fifth graders. They, too, identify strongly with animals and have a sense of kinship with all living things.

Throughout our study, we recall our initial threads: creation and trickster stories, technology and ecology, and how environment shapes culture. We look, again and again, at the multicultural nature of societies; the interaction of humans and the environment; and the culture, geography, and history of diverse societies. And through it all is woven the foundation of social responsibility and the meaning of democracy in how we work with each other on a daily basis.

Whether we are drawing Northwest Coastal animals or learning how to make a cedar canoe with a stone adze, I want the students to appreciate the strength and the ingenuity of these amazing people. I want them to recognize the symbols of the culture so that when later in their lives they see something of Northwest Coastal origin, they will recognize it and have positive feelings about it. One of the reasons I teach is to bring about in my students an openness to different things, ideas, and people. This openness springs from knowledge and appreciation. How else can we make the world a better place?

We replicate Chilkat dancing blankets using the traditional Northwest Coastal design elements—line, ovoid, S and U shapes—and appreciating the symbolism like the hatchmarks of a beaver's tail or the blowhole of a whale. We create coppers and name them using Chinook trade jargon. We try splitting cedar into planks, noting the smell and the feel of this wood so central to the Northwest Coastal people's spirit. We raise salmon and release them into local streams with the help of local Indian fish hatchery personnel, providing an enriched environment that meets the needs of all learning orientations, all intelligences.

Making Books of Knowledge

As a culminating activity, the students make Books of Knowledge, patterned on Indian ledger books from the 1900s. Some Cherokee men were removed from their reservations in Oklahoma and put in a federal penitentiary in Florida because they weren't cooperative. They used ledger books purchased from the prison store to draw pictures of their

Christopher displays his Chilkat blanket.

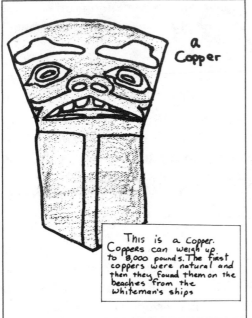

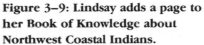

This is a Copper. Coppers can weigh up to 8,000 pounds. The first coppers were natural and then they found them on the beaches from the whiteman's ships

Figure 3–9: Lindsay adds a page to her Book of Knowledge about Northwest Coastal Indians.

history, write notes from their past, and to record chants and songs. Many of these books were destroyed when the men were finally released, but a few have survived, capturing the essence of days now gone.

I want the children to capture a similar essence. Rather than give a final test, I ask the students to demonstrate their knowledge by creating books about Northwest Coastal Indians. They must collect at least twenty things they know about Northwest Coastal life. To tap both sides of the brain, they will draw a picture and describe it in writing, telling about its origin or function (see Figure 3–9). The book must be organized by categories determined by the author, table of contents required, dedication optional. Resources are used in the best possible way—to remind, to verify, to extend. The students do all the work in class. I'm interested in what they know and how they go about their work. They do their initial text in pencil and let me or a peer edit. Some students choose to use the class computer to write their descriptions. (See page 168 in the appendix for a detailed plan for the Book of Knowledge activity.)

It takes a week of concentrated work to complete the task. Everyone is tired, but everyone feels good as arms stretch over heads and backs flex. It feels good because a solid piece of work has been accomplished.

A really worthwhile project is complete. "Is this something you're going to keep to show your own child the kind of work you did in fifth grade?" "YES!"

REFLECTIONS

Powerful social studies is not only integrative in the way topics are treated, but it is also integrative across time and space. Content is linked to past experience and is projected into the future. One of the true strengths of integrating around social studies is that respect for different points of view is encouraged. Multicultural appreciation and awareness is ongoing, an interwoven part of the day, not a unit or a special event to celebrate a holiday.

The mind makes meaning when it sees patterns and relationships. All learners don't make the same meaning, however, nor see the same patterns and relationships. Nevertheless, just by telling my students I'm trying to organize the year so things connect seems to ignite the process of personal integration. We know the mind retains information better when it is placed in a larger context or framework. It seems to me the social studies–integrated classroom is more like real life. It's not terribly tidy, seldom fits into a square box or behind a rectangular desk, and something always seems to come along to modify it.

I love social studies because the students are such an important part of the learning. The dynamic quality of a social studies–integrated classroom has as much to do with the interaction the kids have with the content, with the teacher, and with each other as it does with concept and skill acquisition. It's the social in social studies that makes it so fun to teach. I also love the idea that I can be on Level 1 integration when facilitating our explorer's investigation, approaching Level 4 integration when we study Pacific Northwest Coastal Indians, and at Level 3 during our Inuit work. As my awareness, appreciation, knowledge, and resources grow, my level of integration changes. This keeps teaching dynamic for me and learning exciting for the kids. Who could ever be bored?

Chapter Four

MAKING IT MEANINGFUL

SOCIAL STUDIES TEACHING AND LEARNING
IS POWERFUL WHEN IT IS MEANINGFUL.
—NCSS's *Vision*

Making learning meaningful is the core of teaching. If children don't connect what's going on in the classroom with their minds, their hands, and their hearts, then it seems to me that not much learning is going to occur. How do we know when our teaching and learning is meaningful? Some of the best thinkers and teachers in the National Council for the Social Studies addressed this question and identified elements of meaningful social studies (NCSS 1993, 216):

- ◆ "Rather than memorizing disconnected bits of information or practicing skills in isolation, students learn connected networks of knowledge, skills, beliefs, and dispositions that they will find useful both in and outside of school."
- ◆ "Instruction emphasizes depth of development of important ideas with appropriate breadth of topic coverage and focuses on teaching these important ideas for understanding, appreciation, and life application."
- ◆ "The significance and meaningfulness of the content is emphasized both in how it is presented to students and how it is developed through activities."
- ◆ "Classroom interaction focuses on sustained examination of a few important topics rather than superficial coverage of many."
- ◆ "Meaningful learning activities and assessment strategies focus students' attention on the most important ideas embedded in what they are learning."
- ◆ "The teacher is reflective in planning, implementing, and assessing instruction."

I've observed that what clicks with one learner may leave another confused or frustrated. Therefore, deliberately devising multiple ways for students to experience and demonstrate "knowing" helps me make learning meaningful for all students.

LITERATURE-ENHANCED INSTRUCTION

I'm a little concerned about the intensity of the movement to make literature the base of instruction in the intermediate grades. A strong proponent of using literature to enhance the instruction in our classrooms, I believe balance is the secret, once again. Sometimes, literature leads instruction. The instruction is goal oriented, often chosen for the values it represents or the knowledge it reveals. Sometimes, a concept, skill, or generalization drives learning. Recognition, application, analysis, synthesis, and evaluation guide activities. Literature and the essentials of social studies are almost always blended together to create a whole learning experience for my students. In classrooms in which the story has become the sum of the learning experience, not much social studies learning is accomplished.

INTEGRATION INVITES MEANING

Teaching an integrated curriculum invites meaning. The action in the classroom needs to be meaningful to both the students and the teacher. From our earliest methods classes we've been told that if we, the teachers, act interested then they, the students, will be interested. It seems to me that teachers have to *be* interested, not just *act* interested. The interest, the concern, and the passion of the teacher spill over into the strategies selected to teach the content, choose the resources and materials, allocate time, and communicate expectations.

Teachers not only need to see the connections between content areas, they also have to be willing to push themselves intellectually, physically, and emotionally to find the connections that dispose children to certain knowledge, attitudes, and beliefs. In addition, they need to be open to the connections their students make as well. This kind of collaboration is more powerful than teaching in isolation, more meaningful than confining learning to specific subjects. Disconnected facts and fragmented ideas do little to change the world. Building a network that supports important ideas is critical to today's teacher and learner.

Developing ideas in depth invites the class to spend time not only in investigation and verification, but also in reflection. How content is presented is as important as what is presented. The kinds of activities chosen to apply or reshape information are significant. If the activities are not worthy of the ideas, if the events planned to broaden and deepen understanding trivialize learning, we have shortchanged the learner and sold our own efforts short as well. Meeting goals while considering developmental appropriateness, cost, and feasibility is part and parcel of making learning meaningful.

ESSENTIAL PARTICIPATION SKILLS

When the classroom is connected to the community, meaning is enhanced. To become effective participants, our students need to learn basic participation skills, which include (NCSS 1980):

◆ Working effectively in groups—organizing, planning, making decisions, taking action.
◆ Forming coalitions of interest with other groups.
◆ Persuading, compromising, and bargaining.
◆ Practicing patience and perseverance in working for one's goal.
◆ Developing experience in cross-cultural situations.

INTELLECTUAL ENGAGEMENT

The things we study must matter, must be based on common understanding, and must be approached through worthwhile activities that promote application and encourage independent thinking. Social studies invites multilevel intellectual engagement. There is a rich array of content and ideas to choose from, whether one is focusing on U.S. history or modern Japan. Students can be encouraged to find connections on their own, to develop generalizations to test, and to recognize the "aha's" in their own understanding of how the world works. The beauty of a social studies core is that students do not always have to start with facts before engaging in higher-level thinking. Instead, they can process on several levels at once, relating new knowledge to prior experiences, thinking critically and creatively, or making decisions based on well-founded reasoning (NCSS 1993, 216)

After all these years, Bloom's (1956) taxonomy of cognitive objectives still helps me plan. Working backward from my goals, I constantly check for balance between the applications of concepts, skills, or generalizations. Planning is multidimensional rather than linear. That realization is one of the biggest differences in my planning today compared to when I first started teaching.

"EXPLORERS AND THE EXPLORED"

Teaching Important Ideas

Sometimes I need to teach a unit in a compressed amount of time. Perhaps I've spent too much time on an earlier theme or the way the school calendar is laid out demands it or it's a topic that doesn't need to be dealt with deeply, as long as the important ideas are emphasized. This doesn't happen often, but when it does I make careful choices.

"Explorers" is a topic often included in the fifth-grade curriculum that can be compressed without losing meaning. First, what are the important ideas?

- ♦ More than one point of view about historical "facts."
- ♦ A historical chronology in exploration.
- ♦ Conflicting emotions between the explorer and the explored.
- ♦ Controversy about Christopher Columbus.
- ♦ The dilemma inherent in the word *discovery*.

My goals are for the students to realize there is more than one point of view about historical "facts," to have a notion of when explorations occurred chronologically, to do independent research, and to empathize with the conflicting emotions of the explorer and the explored. There is also controversy about Christopher Columbus and his "discoveries"—can people be discovered?

A class discussion reveals the students have some pretty strong stereotypes about Columbus and some confused notions about other explorers. By way of the lottery box, each student picks an explorer from a list, then spends a short time researching information for a data disk. (See pages 169–170 in the appendix for a detailed plan.) This research is a bit more complex than that for the Inuit data disks. This time the students need to read short factual descriptions that may or may not contain all the desired information. I read aloud stories that share diverse perspectives of Columbus (e.g., Jane Yolen's *Encounter* [1992] and Michael Foreman's *The Boy Who Sailed with Columbus* [1991]). As the students complete their data disks (one is shown in Figure 4–1), we talk about these different perspectives and what they might mean. I read them excerpts from Columbus's log.

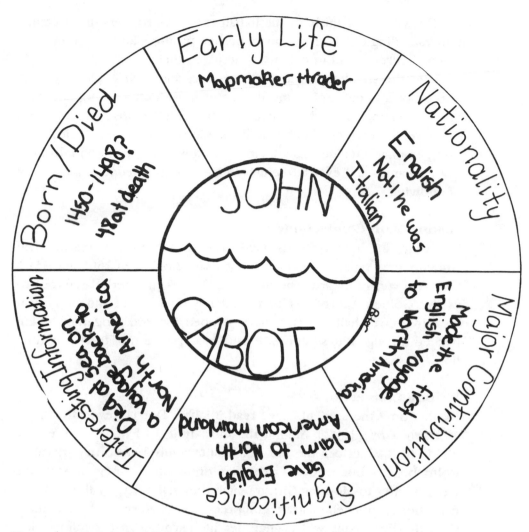

Figure 4–1: Peter's data disk about John Cabot shares important information.

Living Time Line

When the data disks are complete, the students line up in the order of the date of their particular explorer's death. (Death dates more nearly approximate explorations than birth dates do.) The student who researched the explorer who died first stands at the head of the line, the student who researched the last to die goes to the end. The students peek up and down the line, looking at their friends. Each student then introduces his or her explorer and shares information from the data disk, and a living time line of explorers and their explorations is created. (After we finish, we hang the disks in sequence around the border of the room, creating a paper time line we can refer to often.) Identifying the French, the Spanish, or the Italian explorers triggers the students' understanding of which countries pushed frontiers and why they later claimed certain land in colonial America as their own.

Later the students introduce themselves and their explorer to just one other student. Practicing the art of introductions, they mention one interesting thing about their explorer. It's fun and funny. It's the first layer in learning about time lines. Kinesthetic, visual, logical, and interpersonal intelligences are tapped in this strategy. It's an introduction to names and events, the first threads of knowledge in a network of knowing.

Making Math Connections

The time line activity lends itself to a natural math extension. The students who represent explorers who sailed between 1500 and 1599 take two steps forward. The question, Why is this period referred to as the Golden Age of Exploration? takes on graphic and numerical meaning. Over half the class have stepped forward. Cognition is enhanced through kinesthetic and visual manipulation of the living time line.

Writing Connections

By this time the students have read Michael Dorris's evocative book *Morning Girl* (1992). Among the most lyrical of books written for children, it describes the life of a Taino family before the arrival of Columbus. As our study of explorers draws to a close, the students write a letter to Morning Girl in which they tell her what they learned from her story (demonstrate comprehension), alert her how contact with the Europeans will change her life (synthesize the information they gleaned from the reading and research), and share their feelings about what happens to the Taino people (including an affective reaction). Alexa, who has a twin brother and one older brother, wrote:

> Dear Imaginative Morning Girl,
>
> Hi! You've taught me some very interesting things. One truly great thing you taught me is how important brothers and sisters are. The sentence "Without him the silence is very loud" made me realize what a gift my brothers are. You taught me many other things too. But, overall this is the most important.
>
> Boy, did your lives change after contact with explorers and other people who came. Didn't your lives change? From

[what] I heard and learned, you got metal and tools, diseases, etc. The diseases really swept out your villages. I'm sorry!

I have mixed feelings about what happened. I really disagree with the idea of slavery! You aren't a people to be owned by others! You're a kind and gentle group in my opinion. But Europeans and other foreigners did give you useful things. I wish those first explorers would have been nice to you! You were very kind to them, and that proves you are lovable people.

Yours always,
Alexa Nicole

P.S. You've made my imagination stretch!

This letter made me feel as though Alexa had realized the goals for the unit. She was able to discern positive and negative points regarding early exploration. She recognized more than one perspective.

"COLONIAL AMERICA—LIFE, LIBERTY, AND THE PURSUIT OF HAPPINESS"

Reconnecting

To enhance meaning, I try to connect ongoing generalizations and values all year long. As we shift to pre-Revolutionary America, an American Indian thread weaves back into our tapestry of learning. No more do my students experience the "inoculation" principle of learning, "once you've had it, you never get it again." Instead, common threads continue to weave throughout all we study.

The whole class is reading the historical novel *The Double Life of Pocahontas* (Fritz 1983). I read the first chapter while the students follow along and we discuss the contents. I also show a filmstrip and bring in additional books and illustrations. Referring back to the explorer's data disk time line, the class connects exploration to colonization. First, we pinpoint the century Jamestown was created and discuss the gap between Columbus's arrival and the settling of Jamestown. Historical time is a very difficult concept for intermediate-grade children. I encourage the students to develop graphic evidence of chronology by creating pictorial time lines of historical benchmarks that they will be able to use as reference points as they mature. Graphic representations combined with literature are a powerful educational tool. Certainly this pairing is more meaningful than memorizing a list of dates.

The combination is also a very age-appropriate way to create meaningful links during historical studies.

Teaching Each Other

The history of indentured servants is intriguing to fifth graders. The notion of apprentices and master craftsmen is conceptually interesting to ten-year-olds. Using the lottery system again, the students each select a colonial trade to investigate, such as tinsmith, cooper, hat maker, or carpenter. The students use various resources to identify the craft, the tools needed, and the product produced. Each student creates a poster to display his or her research. In addition to a picture of the craftsman at work and a depiction of the tools used, the poster contains a "broadside" advertising for an apprentice in colonial America and a letter to a friend or relative in Europe, as if written by an indentured servant or apprentice working in that trade in the colonies. (See page 171 in the appendix for a detailed plan.)

Why an advertisement? I begin this way because one of the major pieces of study later in the year is how advertising influences choices and decision making, especially when it comes to drugs and alcohol. Our students are bombarded with advertising from the minute they get up and turn on their radio until they click off the television at bedtime. I think students need to understand the techniques of persuasion thoroughly. So I begin gently, asking them to create an ad for an apprentice. This is the first step in becoming aware of propaganda techniques using persuasive writing.

Why letters? I think letters are one of the most interesting forms of communication we have. It's also the form most likely to be used by the students throughout their lifetimes. Letters are often persuasive or informative. They frequently illustrate point of view. Letters let me know what the writer is thinking. I often use letters as a way to check comprehension. I agree with Mem Fox, noted Australian children's author and educator, who writes in her book *Radical Reflections:*

> Isn't it incredible how often writing means writing stories? I can't stand writing stories. Honestly!—What's wrong with letters, for instance? Clarity, voice, power, and control are much more easily developed through letter writing because, perhaps, the audience is so clearly defined and will, if all goes well, respond. (1993, 18)

As the posters go up around the room, the classroom is permeated with interesting information (see the example in Figure 4–2). Exchanges

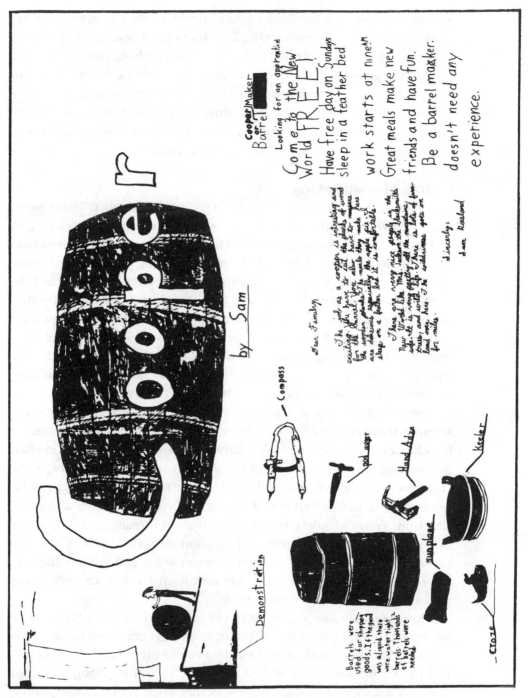

Figure 4–2: Sam's colonial chart is a first try at using posters to teach classmates.

among the students are frequent and lively as they comment or ask questions about each poster. The kids learn from one another as they listen to their peers' presentations and observe how differently each poster is organized. They notice what seems to work. Since this is our first poster piece, we discuss the effectiveness of the students' work and why it is so appealing or informational. The students point out qualitative differences in a positive light. They reveal what they would do again or what they would change next time.

Putting Literature First

As the posters are being created we begin reading Scott O'Dell's *Sarah Bishop* (1980). I especially like this book because both boys and girls find it engaging. It does a good job of bringing out multiple perspectives about the Revolutionary War and provides a setting for the more historically driven information the students will need later to understand the Constitution and the Bill of Rights. Sarah's father is a Tory and suffers abuse because of his beliefs. The threads of witchcraft and religion are also sewn into the fabric of the book. There is a richness to the story that encourages many connections as well as historical scholarship. The whole notion of justice, law, and order is fundamental as well, initiating still another thread we'll continue to follow through the year.

Some teachers may not be comfortable with this selection, however, because there is one episode in which Sam Goshen, a less-than-admirable character, attempts to molest Sarah. She handles the situation effectively and efficiently. Depending on their reading maturity, some children never "get it," and others do. I use the scene to discuss what Sarah does to get herself out of an uncomfortable, possibly dangerous situation. Personal safety is one curriculum we teach, and this seems like a natural place to insert a discussion about it. Today's students certainly need to be well aware of danger signs and what to do, and we need to open up lines of communication so they can talk about uncomfortable things if they need to.

However, it is also important to offer alternatives. We have so many pieces of literature to choose from now that every school topic can be enhanced through more than a single piece of literature. Teachers who feel their community would find the scene in *Sarah Bishop* unacceptable can use other historical novels. Perhaps that is one reason *Johnny Tremain* (Forbes 1943) is often used . I find it rather ponderous and dated, so I show the movie of *Johnny Tremain* instead, and we watch it after reading *Sarah Bishop*. It is a good companion piece, providing a rich series of comparative activities and discussions (Sarah and Johnny, Boston and New York, the Loyalists and the Patriots).

Creating Picture Storyboards

After reading *Sarah Bishop*, we create a storyboard identifying the six elements of a story: main character, setting, situation, problem, conflict, and resolution. (See pages 172–173 in the appendix for a detailed plan and extensions.) The students work in pairs, creating a panel that becomes part of the whole storyboard.

Like all good novels, there are several subplots woven into the main story of *Sarah Bishop*. The students work in groups to present their ideas to the class. Talk centers on the novel and I hear students questioning each other about parts they didn't quite understand or verifying their understanding with a friend. This kind of conversation is rich because it is child centered.

Above the occasional inaccurate assumption or conclusion, I hear children sharing their understanding and insight. I know that children, developmentally, need practice talking about what they read. Like many adults, they often don't really know what they believe until they say it out loud. It seems crucial to me that our students not be judged by the correctness of their responses, but rather by their growth and thoughtfulness in understanding and appreciating literature. By using literature and encouraging conversations enriched with engaging activities, we foster increasingly complex levels of comprehension and appreciation of life through language. My friend Paula Fraser puts it well: "Literature is a way to entice and engage students initially so they are motivated to discover the substance and the facts."

Taking Notes

The hook is in, the kids care. Ready now to gather more factual information, we move to the textbook and other resources, reading to learn. We compare textbook information to the novel *Sarah Bishop* and the movie *Johnny Tremain*. The students meet General Gage, Samuel Adams, John Hancock, Reverend Clark, and Dr. Warren in print. The pieces of colonial life and pre-Revolutionary America connect in meaningful ways.

Philip Spencer wrote a wonderful resource for fifth graders titled *Day of Glory: The Guns at Lexington and Concord* (1955). The book recounts the twenty-four hours surrounding the battles of Lexington and Concord, a chapter for each hour. As the students read through

Dasha and Chris highlight a class storyboard created after reading *Sarah Bishop*, a Revolutionary War story by Scott O'Dell.

the chapters, they record the most interesting information on a paper clock face they've created (see Figure 4–3).

Listening to Unheard Voices

By introducing readings from five different sources, *Black Heroes of the American Revolution* (Davis 1976), *Women of Colonial and Revolutionary America* (Eisenberg 1989), *Founding Mothers: Women of America in Revolutionary Era* (DePauw 1975), *Forgotten Founders* (Johansen 1982), and *Indian Roots of American Democracy* (Barreiro 1988), I ensure that diverse perspectives are visited and validated; that information is extended and enriched; that learning and teaching are meaningful to all students in my classroom, not just to a favored few; that cultural connections and ethnic origins are recognized and studied. This is not accidental but deliberate and is guided by my personal belief that historical studies should be inclusive. In the past, textbooks and other easily accessible materials have tended to be monocultural. Nowadays, there may be a mention or two of minority contributions, but it is more often tokenism than anything else. If we truly value a pluralistic

society, we must provide more than passing mention of the roles diverse people played in our past.

In my classroom, valuing multicultural America permeates the day, week, month, and year. It is not something I teach for a week or two. I don't do a multicultural unit. Instead, over the years, a learning environment has developed that touches, recognizes, and values the diversity of our classroom and our community. We don't "do" Indians on Thanksgiving and African Americans on Martin Luther King Day. Ethnic literature, games, and songs fill the classroom all year. I've moved away from the Tacos-on-Tuesday Syndrome, a term coined by Mako Nakagawa. A multicultural education specialist formerly with the Washington State Office of the Superintendent of Public Instruction, Mako was referring to those classrooms whose total multicultural education program consists of recognizing a culture (e.g., Mexican) in a one-day celebration centering around food (e.g., tacos). While food is important, certainly there is more to cultural understanding than a single dish. Certainly understanding a culture takes more than single day.

91

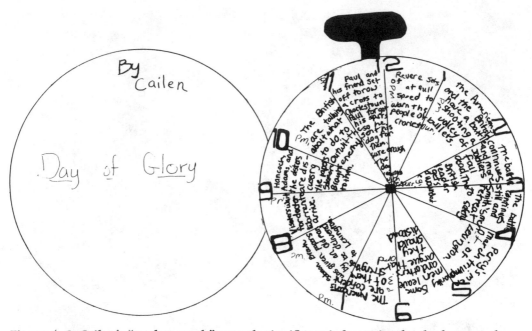

Figure 4–3: Cailen's "pocket watch" records significant information by the hour as she reads *Day of Glory*.

Presenting a Microlecture

Picture the poor patriots—broke, disorganized, and basically alone. Small-scale riots and neighbors harboring grudges against each other. What is this fledgling country to do?—*If You Were There When They Signed the Constitution* (Levy 1987) is a quick read-aloud to set the stage for more learning. What would you do? Get a group of respected people together and work out the problem. Does it seem logical? It does to the kids. Why weren't there American Indians, women, Hispanics, or African Americans involved? The students know. They are familiar with colonial society.

Not having a particularly engaging resource for the students to read about the "founding fathers" and the history of the events leading to the actual gathering in Philadelphia, I decide to use a microlecture. Seldom more than ten minutes in length, the microlecture is a strategy I choose when nothing else is as effective or efficient. I usually use it when there aren't any appropriate student materials available and/or when there is little time in which to disseminate the information. I make sure my presentation is upbeat, interesting, and accurate. I model the elements of engaging public presentations. My goal is to inform quickly by pointing out specific steps or identifying key elements.

Practicing Taking Tests

During our study of Revolutionary America, facts, concepts, and generalization are woven into a comprehensible pattern. At the close of our study, we are ready to practice test taking. There's a certain amount of specific information students need to have at hand about the colonial period. I am particularly interested in their understanding of the events leading to the Revolutionary War. It's important for them to be aware of the issues involved. We start with a review. Using a study guide and working in groups, the kids think it's fun. Their interaction is lively and focused. They can ask anyone for assistance. But they have to assist someone else before they can request help again. The process jogs memories and encourages students to share their interpretations of what we have read, viewed, and discussed. Believing laughter stimulates the memory, I encourage humor as we work. Learning should be fun!

Setting a tone for collaboration among the students, their parents, and me, I alert the parents to our "examination." We have discussions in class to clear up any confusion or misunderstanding. Study buddies are selected and time is provided for shared studying. I never test on Monday. Sunday evenings are too precarious for many students. The test is Tuesday. We are ready. The students are focused, serious, and intent. This is practice in self-discipline. And I want every student to win. Knowing quantifiable information is a valid activity, but certainly not an end in itself.

In addition to recalling a few facts, the students have an opportunity to show their understanding of cause and effect, their grasp of relationships, and their ability to predict what might have happened if a different verdict had been found at the Peter Zenger trial or King George had been of a different character. The most creative part of the test is a takeoff on—*If You Lived in Colonial Times* (McGovern 1964). Choosing one of several hypothetical scenarios, the students write what their lives would have been like.

I grade these paper-and-pencil tests quickly, using scoring we've agreed on beforehand. (See Chapter 8 for a discussion of assessment strategies.) I show the class how I read the papers and what I think as I score their papers. I invite the kids to share their reactions. We talk about why one answer "works" and another doesn't. They figure the mean, median, and mode. In essence, I try to demystify testing for my students unlocking traditional, almost genetic, test phobias. Haven't you had parents tell you they aren't surprised that Johnny can't do math or social studies because "I was always awful in math" or "I never liked history"? Instead, my students have a model for test preparation, test taking, and test evaluation. Testing in a supportive, happy environment occurs several times throughout the year, until every child feels confident.

Ending with a Song

The students have a solid understanding of colonial times, Revolutionary War issues, and the people and events important to that historic period. Now we need to synthesize and personalize it into a whole. Music is one way to do it. Gary Chalk has written a wonderful book titled *Yankee Doodle: A Revolutionary Tail* (1993). In it, he has written his own lyrics summarizing the events surrounding the Revolution, to the tune of "Yankee Doodle," a song associated with that time. His verses deal with things like taxes, the Boston Tea Party, the Minutemen and Paul Revere, the shot heard 'round the world, Bunker Hill, the Declaration of Independence, Hessians, Washington crossing the Delaware, and the first Stars and Stripes, to mention a few. I use the pictures in the book and a few of Chalk's verses to familiarize the students with the tune and the form. Then we brainstorm all the possible events, people, and issues. The children, working alone or in small groups, create their own verses and write them on overhead transparencies. Many draw scenes to accompany their lyrics. When everyone is ready, each verse is placed on the overhead and we all sing and laugh and share our knowledge.

Piecing It Together

Quilting, a common craft in colonial times, is quite engaging to intermediate-grade students. While I once had a student's mother come in and teach quilting to my students, I am more pulled to the color and form of quilts than to the stitchery. We usually create personal quilts out of paper. (See page 174 in the appendix for detailed plans.) We begin by looking at quilt patterns and listening to quilting stories. *Eight Hands Round* (Paul 1991) is an especially delightful quilt book because each page gives a brief history of the pattern, shows one square in detail, and then shows a series of squares so the overall pattern is apparent. The mathematical repetition of quilting is intriguing. The memories and history of the fabric that makes up a quilt evokes wonder and special feelings.

After looking at and talking about quilt designs, color, and form, my students each create a personal quilt. Felt-tip markers make bright, sharp colors. Colored pencils bring a soft, pastel feeling to the design. Colored crayons add texture. Using paper lightly lined in one-inch squares, the students create their own memory quilt. I encourage them to draw on knowledge as well as experience to fill in their squares. Some choose to make a series of one-inch designs, others work in four-inch or nine-inch patterns. Math applications occur as the student use symmetry, fractions, and tessellations. We've discovered over the years that outlining each square with a solid color brings out the design more clearly. Children are urged to share their designs: "piggybacking" is the best form of flattery. The quilts project wraps up our colonial study by appealing to the kinesthetic and the visual, locking in memories and providing a vehicle for self-expression. When the students are finished, I laminate their work because the process heightens and intensifies the colors. It also protects the project until it reaches home. So much work and careful detail needs to be ensured safe passage. (Lizzie's quilt is used on the cover of this book.)

REFLECTIONS

I think intermediate-grade students need to experience learning with all of their intelligences. While teachers may not need to teach through every single intelligence every single day, we should provide an environment that encourages children to explore or expand their own learning orientations. Multiple ways to become knowledgeable as well as multiple ways to demonstrate knowing mean that more children will experience success.

Teachers who incorporate the multiple intelligences into their planning use words like *networks, connections, sustained, authentic,* and *reflections.* Students *read, participate, relate, write, invent, design, interpret, construct, chart, illustrate, describe, conduct, demonstrate, generate, laugh,* and *share.* This kind of vocabulary characterizes meaningful teaching and learning. Integrating parts and fashioning them together makes it possible for children to experience their education wholly.

Jesse Jackson, in his speech to the 1988 Democratic Convention, said that "America's not a blanket woven from one thread, one color, one cloth." He went on to say that sewing together pieces of cloth, patches of wool, silk, and gabardine, with sturdy hands and strong cord creates a quilt, "a thing of beauty, power, and culture." The fabric of our country is made up of individual and unique pieces, just as our classrooms are made up of individual and unique students. Together, these pieces form a strong cloth that will wave forever. Ours are the hands, our planning the cord, that contribute to the character and knowledge of our students. Acknowledging, appreciating, and accommodating individual differences within our classrooms makes learning meaningful.

Chapter Five

EXPLORING VALUES AND POINTS OF VIEW

SOCIAL STUDIES TEACHING AND LEARNING
IS POWERFUL WHEN IT IS VALUE-BASED.
—NCSS's *Vision*

MAKING MULTIPLE PERSPECTIVES REAL

Gary Howard, director of the Respecting Our Ethnic and Cultural Heritage (REACH) Center, likes to explain the concept of multiple perspectives this way: he describes an accident occurring at the intersection of five streets. On one corner stands a young man who has recently been arrested for driving under the influence and has had his license revoked. On a second corner stands an elderly woman with cataracts who has never had a driver's license. On the third corner is a middle-aged career woman hurrying to an appointment. On the fourth corner is a recent immigrant who is used to driving on the left-hand side of the road. A trained insurance investigator stands on the fifth corner. How do you think their stories might differ when each is asked to describe the accident? Their point of view—where they were physically at the moment of the accident as well as their awareness, their interest, their own past experiences, their knowledge, and their ability to describe what they saw accurately—will influence each story. This is what multiple perspectives are about, and it is an incredibly important concept to teach children.

Those who teach nine- to twelve-year-olds know just how egocentric they are. It has never occurred to many of these children that they are not the center of the universe. Nearly every event is personalized. Almost all action is a stimulus or response to self-gratification—not in a greedy or grasping way, but in a naive, unconscious way. Yet intermediate-grade children also are openly sensitive to the plight of others, want to rescue the weak and protect the innocent, are masters of righteous indignation. Their sense of justice is highly developed and the worst epithet that they can utter is, "It isn't fair."

Literature brings multiple perspectives to life in the classroom better than any other resource I know. Diverse perspectives are most vividly realized through narrative, whether legend, folktale, novel, or true story.

Children need to connect with heretofore unexamined issues, unexplored thoughts, and unexplained rationales. Caught up in a story, we care about the characters and experience their problems vicariously. The bond between reader and story creates a friendly foundation for age-appropriate discussions, debates, simulations, and research.

UNEARTHING ETHICAL DIMENSIONS

Opening children up to other perspectives is one of the most delightful tasks a teacher has. Kids are so adept at learning how to look at issues from more than one side. Paradoxically, they are not so quick to apply the notion of multiple perspectives if the issue involves them. One of the true strengths of powerful social studies teaching is that it encourages respect for opposing points of view, sensitivity to cultural differences, and a commitment to social responsibility and action (NCSS 1993, 218).

Recognizing that it's easier to talk about something than it is to do it, the democratic classroom encourages students to apply multiple perspectives, not just give lip service to the concept. Considering the ethical dimensions of topics can become a routine part of learning. Controversial issues can be addressed maturely and readily. The realization that anything can be talked about leads to deeper reflection and more engaged ways of being in the real world.

The classroom should be a safe forum for trying out ideas and suggesting solutions. The teacher's role is to encourage the students to respect the dignity and rights of others while ideas are being tested and shared. Teaching children the language of multiple perspectives is necessary at this age—"some people think this way, other people think that way." Sharing strategies with them for weighing the costs and benefits of choices is an important part of value-based teaching. Through the teacher's questioning and modeling, students begin to internalize basic democratic concepts and principles when making personal decisions or finding solutions to public problems. Surrounded by people who demonstrate they care about the common good engenders an environment for prosocial values and social responsibility.

Justin enjoys trying out new ideas and finding interesting solutions.

Intermediate-grade students are ready to look at the implications of social action and to think critically about social issues. Too often, there isn't enough time to examine persistent social issues in our classrooms. The integrated curriculum buys the time we need to identify and analyze relevant information about an issue, to measure the merits of various arguments, and to make thoughtful, reasoned decisions.

ACHIEVING BALANCE

As teachers, we need to be keenly aware of our own values. We need to think about how these values affect the teaching strategies we use, the resources we suggest, and the questions we ask. Then we need to adjust our planning to achieve balance. Our responsibility is to make sure the students are aware of the many points of view inherent in an issue. Our students should remain unaware of our personal views on an issue, at least while we are studying it together. We should help children identify the positive and negative attributes of decisions. Weighing the advantages and disadvantages is an important undertaking at this time in a child's development.

Once again, how we do something is as important as what we do. Promoting positive human relationships while acknowledging opposing perspectives models mature behavior. Demonstrating respect for well-reasoned positions rather than accepting shoot-from-the-lip responses helps children develop a more critical habit of mind. Displaying sensitivity to cultural differences and similarities validates every child in the room. Demonstrating a willingness to compromise, to listen carefully, and to search for the common good provides a springboard for student reflection and subsequent positive behavior. The notion of perspective nudges children toward a deeper understanding of themselves and others. It begins the process of empathy and sets students up to become "bigger than themselves," to live more widely than their young lives can allow. Looking at multiple perspectives at this age is incredibly freeing. Seeing two, three, or more sides to an issue is evidence of growth, intellectually and emotionally.

STRATEGIES FOR SEEING MORE THAN ONE SIDE

In our classrooms, we can make it a point to expose students to multiple perspectives. We can give children an opportunity to experience multiple ways of looking at knowledge. The very strategies we choose to use in our classrooms convey our appreciation for diversity. Providing formats that encourage students to share their own perspectives help our students grow.

Story Ladders
New year, new beginnings! As a transition to new studies, we begin *The Forgotten Door*, a story by Alexander Key (1965) about a boy from an alien planet who falls through a forgotten door into Ozark hill country in early 1950. He is treated with suspicion and irrational hatred by some and with sympathy and support by others, according to their conflicting points of view. Using a strategy I call the story ladder, I ask the students to depict the four most important parts of the story. (See page 175 in the appendix for a detailed plan.) Most interesting is the way one child will use mostly words and sketchy pictures, while another will choose pictures only. Each is effective. Each is affective. Both demonstrate unique yet shared interpretations of the story.

Law, Literature, and Point of View
The Forgotten Door features a courtroom scene. I like to extend our exploration of different points of view into law-related education strate-

gies and hold a mock hearing. While I personally am not interested in scripted trials, I do find simulations in which the students develop the sworn statements for the witnesses, research points of view, and play the parts accurately very exciting. Certainly, values and opinions are brought out in an orderly and predictable way. The students in these kinds of simulations practice higher-order thinking as they question, analyze, and respond to thoughtful questions by the opposition.

Historical Context

While many students have had an opportunity to learn about Martin Luther King, Jr., it is usually fifth grade when what they know is placed in a historical context. So often, we "do" the Civil War but leave African Americans enslaved in children's minds, treat great black leaders as anomalies rather than the norm.

I like to introduce civil rights in my classroom immediately after we study the Constitution and the Bill of Rights. While King's birthday frequently accents our study, it is not treated as a one-day spectacular. Instead, we investigate ideas the kids have about violations of rights. Inevitably, a child will cite racism or segregation as a civil rights violation. With that impetus, we begin our study.

I like to begin with King's stirring words. Each student memorizes a small section of one of his many memorable speeches. Then we present an oral ABC of Martin Luther King, Jr. Each child repeats words this great man spoke about concepts ordered alphabetically (All together, Brotherhood, Cooperation, etc.). We spend time looking at the issues and events that inspired the words. We investigate the meaning of the words and appreciate the way in which he used language. We practice delivering the words in a way he would have admired, enjoying the solemnity and grandeur of the English language. We identify issues he would probably be involved with today. And as we sing "We Shall Overcome," I hope the students will remember this ten years from now, standing hand in hand, reviving old promises and making new ones about life, liberty, and the pursuit of happiness for all.

Literary License

Moving on to the Civil War, we start with literature. We begin by studying slavery and the Underground Railroad prior to the Civil War. Civil rights, the Civil War, and slavery are topics rich in values and points of view. They are a source to be mined as the children try on different perspectives and learn the language of opposing viewpoints.

All the kids read the same historical novel, *The Story of Harriet*

101

Tubman: Freedom Train, by Dorothy Sterling (1954). They compare it with information in the social studies textbook and other resources about Harriet Tubman. They verify or repudiate the information in conflict within their expanding repertoire of historical issues and events. They discuss the notion of "license" in historical fiction, finding examples and hypothesizing why the author chose to illuminate some information accurately and other information not as accurately.

Letters from the Heart of History

I think it is the combination of scholarship and appreciation for conflicting points of view that reaches to the heart of history and touches the mind of the intermediate-grade learner. Writing helps us know what we think and think about what we know. Letters are one of the most age-appropriate and engaging strategies I use to encourage my students to reveal their knowledge and engage in personal reflection (see page 176 in the appendix for a detailed plan).

When we begin reading the novel about Tubman, the children choose a character in the book and write about Harriet to a friend as if they were that character. Meghann, as the plantation owner's wife, Mrs. Sara, writes the letter below after reading the first three chapters:

> Dear MoJo,
>
> My husband has died, and I have to take care of the slaves. They are all stubborn but there is one slave named Harriet that I particularly hate. She is extremely stubborn and will not listen to me. A while ago she was somewhere and got hit in the head with a 2 lb. weight and ever since she's had sleeping spells.
>
> I think she is useless and is a cheap excuse for a slave. She is strong but terribly useless with all those sleeping spells. I cannot afford all the slaves so I think I will get rid of her.
>
> Harriet will probably be sold to a cotton plantation in the south. If I don't sell her, I will get no money and [she] will probably run away. I hope people will buy her even though she has sleeping spells. Hope to see you soon but so long for now.
>
> Sincerely yours,
> Mrs. Sara

Further along in the reading, the kids change perspectives, writing as Harriet to some other character. Meghann writes as Harriet communicating with William Still, a Quaker conductor on the Underground Railroad:

Dear William,

How are you? Can you remember the first time we met? I can. I was looking at the Liberty Bell but I could not read it. So I looked around and there was a proud looking man so I asked him If he could read the bell to me. That man was you.

I can remember my first journey to the north and how so many people helped me. It was cold but I kept on moving. I can also remember the day my own [master] died and how we were all afraid of being sold.

It's weird but I feel like Moses because I also lead my people to freedom. But the one main difference is I can't part water. I am going to keep on doing what I am doing now but It's getting harder to take them all the way up to Canada. I hope to see you soon.

Sincerely yours,
Harriet Tubman

Finally, after finishing the book, they write to Harriet from today, as themselves, telling her what they admire most about her, what she'd find surprising today, and what she might do if she were here now. Here is Erik's letter to Harriet Tubman:

February 1, 1991

Dear Harriet Tubman,

Hi! I'm Erik R. I live on Mercer Island, Washington, which is a free state like the other 50 states. I'm writing to you from the future. I'm 11 years old and in fifth grade. After you stopped leading people out of slavery, I liked the way you helped more people as a nurse.

I think that if you were living now you would be very interested in all the stuff we do by computer. If you are wondering what a computer is it is a machine that helps you do things without as much hassle. For example, I'm writing you this on a computer. Even though I think you would like that, I think you would be disappointed that the U.S.A. (United States of America) and another country called Iraq are having a war. Iraq is trying to boss around smaller countries that are close to Iraq like Kuwait.

If you were alive today the kind of work you would most want to do is government work. This means you could help our country stay together, kind of like Abraham Lincoln.

Sincerely,
Erik R.

Exploring Values and Points of View

Darby and Alyssa create a poem for two voices.

Poetry with a Purpose

"Poems for Two Voices" is a technique for revealing what I call the "smart heart," the combining of knowing and feeling. This strategy encourages the children to respect others and illuminates their ability to incorporate basic democratic concepts and principles into their own lives. Marj Montgomery, of Day Junior High in Newton, Massachusetts, first shared this idea with me in 1988, using Paul Fleischman's *Joyful Noise: Poems for Two Voices* as a model. (See page 177 in the appendix for a detailed plan.) Pairs of students write a joint poem, a dialogue for two opposing points of view. Each voice speaks individually, but the two voices also speak together, offering comments about which they agree or about which they agree to disagree. Luke and Sarah wrote the following poem for two voices after reading the book about Harriet Tubman. The characters are Thomas Garret, a Quaker, and Daddy Ben, Harriet Tubman's father.

THOMAS GARRET	BOTH CHARACTERS TOGETHER	DADDY BEN
	Why does the color of our skin matter?	
I'm white.		
		I'm black.
	We both love the thought of freedom for each and every person.	
Our worlds are separate.		
		But just as equal.
Why should skin matter?		
		The color of your eyes don't matter.
The color of your hair does not matter.		
		We both work long hard hours.
I get paid for what I do.		
		I don't get a single dime.
	Why does the color of our skin matter?	

INVESTIGATING PERSONAL PERSPECTIVES

When I want to focus on a single perspective, I use a strategy called "interior monologues," which I also learned from Marj Montgomery. To introduce this integrative strategy (see page 178 in the appendix for a detailed plan) I ask the class if they ever have conversations inside their heads. The students are often surprised to find out they aren't the only ones who "head talk." We discuss how interior monologues give us incredible freedom to hop around mentally from idea to idea and provide a way to practice how we will express ourselves in public. The students then write as if they were a character in the book carrying on an interior monologue. Jon wrote the following as if he were Jim, the slave Harriet tried to protect from the overseer's brutality. Instead she was permanently injured.

> I really wish I was the one that got hit by that two lb. weight instead of Harriet. She doesn't deserve to have sleeping spells, but I do. Please let me suffer and not Harriet. Gosh Harriet you shouldn't have held me—then again maybe it was sort of her fault, too—what am I thinking it was all my fault. I should have stayed at the master's plantation and gone without to-bacco or told Harriet to stay and not to warn me, but I think Harriet will do just fine—or she might be sold "down river." Oh Harriet, how I wish you had stayed at the plantation be-cause I can take a whipin' and keep on tickin'—Oh, Harriet—Oh, Harriet you foolish girl, you.

BLENDING RESEARCH, RESOURCES, AND LITERATURE

In this unit, the students also investigate the lives of Lincoln and Davis. As we did when we studied the Revolutionary War, we try to identify issues. We compare life in the North with life in the South. We look at the geography, the economy, and the society of Northerners and Southerners. Sometimes we draw megamaps, large-scale representations of the eastern third of the United States. These maps are approximate rather than precise. We do them as pictorial representations rather than replicas. Locating strategic places and identifying important sites helps keep history grounded.

At the same time, the children are reading Civil War novels. Two favorites are Jean Fritz's *Brady* (1960) and William O. Steele's *The Perilous Road* (1958). The books are written from different points of view, the former from the Northern perspective and the latter from the Southern. The students enjoy acting out conversations between Brady, a Northerner who didn't figure he had any obligation toward slaves, and Chris, the central character in *The Perilous Road*, who is a Yankee-hating Confederate. These conversations are always quite spon-taneous, and we stage them at least three times while the children are reading the books. This allows me to monitor their comprehension of the characters and the issues. (See page 179 in the appendix for a detailed plan.)

REPORTING FROM A BIAS

During reading workshop, we learn more about different perspectives from various resources. As our study of the Civil War draws to a close, we turn once again to the newspaper. This time the class is divided into three groups. One group is designated Southern Whites, another, Northern Whites, a third, Free Blacks. Each group is responsible for creating a newspaper from their specific point of view. The groups each choose an editor, who then assigns reporters a specific space to fill and kind of article to write. (See pages 180–181 in the appendix for detailed plans.) The variety of writing within a newspaper—editorials, news reports, special features, religion, sports, horoscope, obituaries, comics, classified ads, crosswords, puzzles, political cartoons, and advertising— makes it possible for every child to contribute positively to the group work. It is also imperative that each child *does* contribute or the paper will be incomplete.

The editor checks each article and sends the reporter back to rewrite if necessary. In less than a week, the papers, culminating the children's study of the Civil War, are hanging in the room. Each group reads their paper to the rest of the class. I hear the generalizations, check the facts, and have a very good idea of what the children know, what they can do, and how they feel about the Civil War and the people of that period.

Stacy, Dan, and Julia display perspective newspapers from the Civil War.

Exploring Values and Points of View

INVESTIGATING IMMIGRATION

Our next focus of study is usually immigration. Our region is particularly influenced by Asian immigration, so we compare the Asian American experiences on Angel Island with European American experiences on Ellis Island. I often read *Journey to Topaz,* by Yoshiko Uchida (1971) aloud to the class. This book helps students understand institutionalized racism through the story of a Japanese American family in Berkeley, California, at the time of Pearl Harbor. Just as many children know nothing about the Holocaust, many know nothing about internment. Every year I have Japanese American children in my classroom, and some of them know little about internment, either. Just because children are of a particular race, teachers cannot assume they are historically literate.

It's easy to move from fiction to nonfiction by sharing the history of Gordon Hirobayashi. He is one of three Japanese Americans who refused to follow Executive Order 9066, which required all Japanese Americans to keep a curfew and to relocate to camps inland during World War II. His experience connects to our study of civil rights. Gordon Hirobayashi, born and raised in the Seattle area, was a University of Washington student when he was incarcerated. Later, he took his lawsuit through the courts to the Ninth Circuit Court of Appeals in Seattle.

We recreate another courtroom scene. This time our knowledge base is not literature but real life and primary documents. It is important to make sure the students understand the tenor of the times. The children study photocopies of Executive Order 9066. We read archival copies of newspapers and diaries of internees. We view old newsreels and watch videos depicting America during World War II. We discuss the courage it takes to stand up for what is right. The students culminate their study with a time line of Gordon Hirobayashi's life, created in a coloring-book format. We print a copy of the complete coloring book for each child to take home and share with his or her family. (Figures 5–1 and 5–2 are pages from the book.)

POPPING UP WITH POP-UP BOOKS

The thread of justice continues to weave throughout our studies all year long. In connection with our immigration theme, the whole class often reads *In the Year of the Boar and Jackie Robinson,* by Bette Bao Lord (1984). This story of a Chinese girl who immigrates to Brooklyn

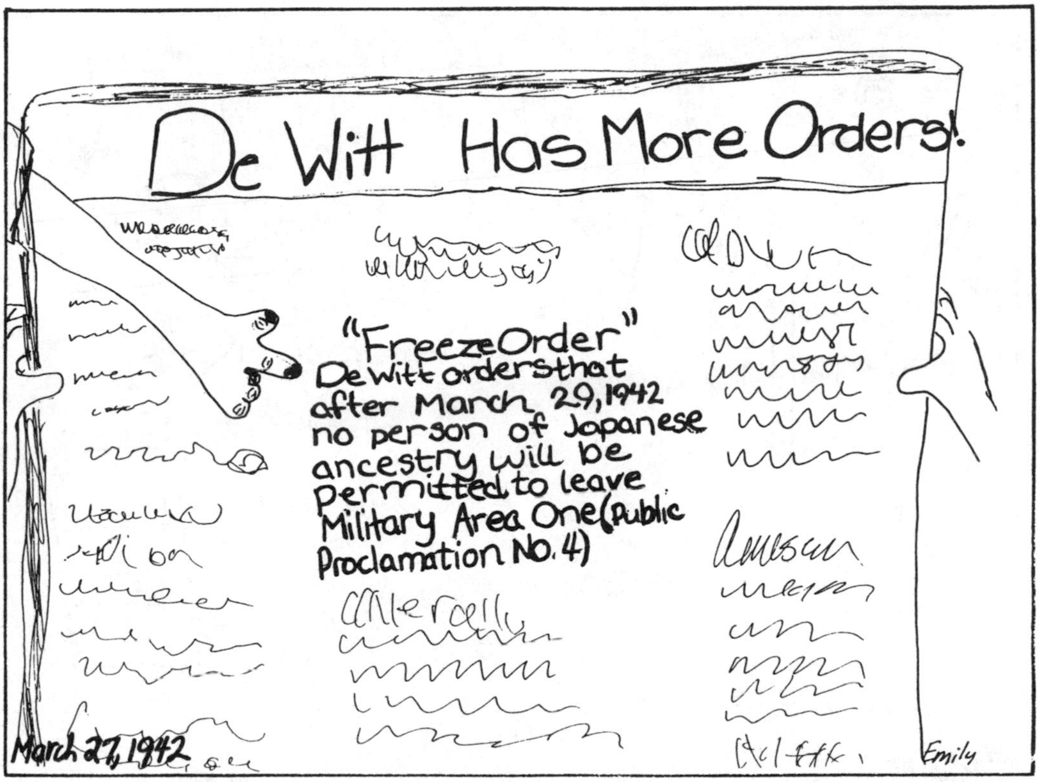

Figure 5–1: Emily's contribution to the Gordon Hirobayashi time line.

in 1947 is perfect for the spring—baseball season is about to begin. The students already have a good grounding in immigration. Now they meet a girl who tells about her confusion with English, her misunderstandings at school, her friendships, and her family. Is it a variation of the theme in *The Forgotten Door*? Maybe. That's also for the students to determine. But one strong message is that America is the land where dreams can come true, where people of all races can find freedom and justice. Is that true? Maybe. That's for the students to determine.

It's time for a really kinesthetic activity. The students make pop-up books highlighting each chapter of *In the Year of the Boar and Jackie Robinson*. Using *How to Make Pop-Ups* by Joan Irvine (1987), the students depict their comprehension in a new format. The tie-in with Jackie Robinson weaves back to our civil rights study begun in January. The picture books *Teammates*, by Peter Golenbach (1990), a story about Jackie Robinson and Pee Wee Reese and *Baseball Saved Us*, by Ken Mochizuki (1993), a story about a boys' baseball team in an internment camp, bring us to a sense of closure. By gathering and analyzing information and assessing the merits of diverse points of view,

Exploring Values and Points of View

Figure 5–2: Allison's contribution to the Gordon Hirobayashi time line.

the students become more aware of social policy decisions, like internment and desegregation. They begin to demonstrate the ability to think critically as they explain reasons for their decisions and their solutions.

DEALING WITH DIFFICULT ISSUES

A Vision of Powerful Teaching and Learning in the Social Studies presents three steps to include when dealing with difficult issues in the classroom. Teachers should make sure that students:

1. Become aware of values, complexities, and dilemmas involved in an issue
2. Consider the costs and benefits to various groups that are embedded in potential courses of actions, and
3. Develop well-reasoned positions consistent with basic democratic social and political values. (NCSS 1993, 217)

They then can be confident that they've provided sound guidance regarding value-based decision making in a democratic classroom.

REFLECTIONS

Layer upon layer, thread intertwining with thread, what we know and how we feel permeates the pattern of our lives. It is our responsibility to give students the opportunity to become aware and informed about diverse points of view. We need to help them discover that solutions reflect values. We need to provide them avenues for exploring their own personal values as well as those of a democratic society. Developmentally, our students are moving from self-centeredness to other-centeredness—physically, intellectually, and emotionally. They need frameworks for making decisions. Learning to assess the costs and benefits of a plan of action, whether public or private, is smart. Practicing in the classroom predisposes students to use a similar decision-making model when not in the classroom.

Becoming aware that different people may see the same event or issue in very different ways is often a revelation for the intermediate-grade student. Connecting their behavior on the playground (Why am I always in trouble?) to the classroom (Let's weigh costs and benefits. Let's look at that from someone else's point of view) is as far removed from our students' comprehension as the Civil War was prior to our study, unless we provide the connections. We are the cord that connects content to self-knowledge. We shape the student as a citizen of today's classroom and tomorrow's world.

Exploring Values and Points of View

Chapter Six

ACTIVATING LEARNING

SOCIAL STUDIES TEACHING AND LEARNING
IS POWERFUL WHEN IT IS ACTIVE.

—NCSS's *Vision*

When I started teaching thirty years ago, my desk was front and center; the children's desks faced it in neat little rows. I was the star and they were the audience. These days my desk is in the back of the room, where it is used for storing things in, putting things on, and hiding things under. Since I have started integrating the curriculum around social studies, I find I no longer have to carry the whole responsibility of teaching and learning. Sometimes I teach, sometimes my students teach. We all learn. Learning is as much my student's responsibility as it is mine. In fact, one of the most interesting things I've observed is how my students and I gradually shift roles over a course of study. They wean themselves away from my authority and become autonomous learners. I laughingly call this the bonbon approach to teaching, after those moments when the students are so intent in their own investigations that I feel I really could put my feet up and eat bonbons while the children carry on independently.

When children are investigating genuine questions, ones that neither they nor I know the answer to, I have as much to learn as they. Open-ended activities that have the flexibility to extend student knowledge in areas of real interest enrich both teacher and students.

PLANNING, PLANNING, PLANNING

Planning is crucial in creating a balanced and worthwhile educational experience for children. I look at my whole year as one long focus on social studies. That way, I don't feel forced to get everything in one

113

unit. I have the flexibility to dip deeply into content. Making curricular plans and adjustments leads to active teaching and learning in the social studies. Deliberate connections among content, concepts, and skills will ingrain the knowing, doing, and feeling so crucial to the kind of education I have come to value.

Planning has many components. One often overlooked is the need always to update our own knowledge and understanding of the learning process. Knowing what to teach and how to teach it requires frequent self-analysis and exposure to other ideas and strategies. That's why I belong to professional organizations like our Washington State Council for the Social Studies and the National Council for the Social Studies. Attending conferences, participating in seminars, volunteering to serve on districtwide educational committees, and reading widely activates me and my teaching.

MEETING MULTIPLE LEARNING STYLES

We know that children don't always get stuff when they are told. Education is not a process of being stuffed. Instead, it is an active process inviting children to explore, to question, and to verify. Social studies is very rich. There's so much to get into. Children need to make sense of what they are learning by manipulating information, investigating questions, checking what they know, and identifying what they don't know.

The activities teachers plan for students can greatly enhance this learning process or impede it. Activities that rely on rote work seldom bring great rewards. Activities that encourage students to develop individual expertise, construct a cooperative group project, or modify an inaccurate belief are much more effective. An activity that helps a child gain self-confidence is a good activity. One that nurtures creativity, spotlights strengths, or eases a child down an intellectual, physical, or emotional path not taken before is a very good activity indeed. And I think we get more bang for our buck when those activities are connected.

Active learning and teaching are multifaceted. It seems to me that teachers who are interested in multiple intelligences should direct their own creativity and problem-solving abilities toward establishing integrated learning in their classrooms. As a teacher, I love the challenge of trying to devise useful, worthwhile, stimulating, connected opportunities for students "to apply existing knowledge to questions about new content, to learn new content with understanding, to synthesize and communicate what they have learned, to generate new knowledge or creative applications, or to think critically about the content and make decisions or take actions that relate to it" (NCSS 1993, 219).

We should not engage students in artificial activities. You know the kind I mean, the ones when the students look up at you after completing the assignment, a big "So what?" in their eyes. I think activities should matter. They should invite the student to develop a social understanding applicable to the real world around them. They should have an opportunity to "try on" new modes of behavior, whether it is watching a television advertisement critically or volunteering to work with the kindergarten students during recess.

LEARNING ABOUT RESEARCH WRITING

A common language arts goal in the intermediate grades is to provide experience and develop skills in research writing. Rather than invite the students to choose any topic they wish, I prefer to focus their research and their writing on subjects connected to social studies. The students have had quite a bit of practice extrapolating data from various resources by using the data disk. Now it is time to move to a second layer of complexity: the data sheet. Data sheets are organizers I developed several years ago to help all children in my classroom write research papers successfully. I have always had several children on individualized education plans (IEPs), many of them identified as attention deficient disabled or learning disabled. I feel that too often students are asked to do research but are not given the support needed to develop a lifelong strategy. Data sheets are my attempt to give all learners a process that will be reliable and replicable. (See pages 182–185 in the appendix for models.)

After we've modeled how to use the data sheets in connection with an exercise using a general topic and the encyclopedia, I ask my students to choose one of the original thirteen colonies to research. They may work with a partner or alone, but each student needs to discuss some of the general, cultural, and economic aspects of the chosen colony. Some decide to use the computer so they can make corrections easily. Others decide to handwrite. We set up a time line of due dates, so that the students will be able to manage their time more easily. I expect the work to be done in class and give enough time for it to be completed. This is not homework. It's important in-class work. I want to be able to supervise and support each student as they try out their research "wings." (Pages 186 and 187 in the appendix show a suggested assignment sheet and a possible assessment rubric.)

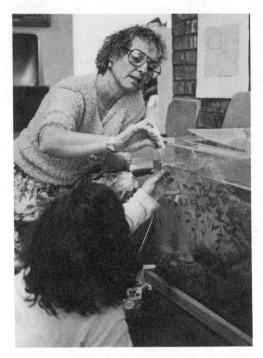

Raising salmon in the classroom integrates science with civics.

INTEGRATING CIVICS AND SCIENCE

Perhaps no single topic lends itself more readily to active, connected, and purposeful activities than environmental education. I have trouble seeing environmental education as a science-only issue. I find there is a civics side to the environment that puts it squarely into the social studies arena as well. Anyway, for a teacher in a self-contained integrated classroom, it doesn't really matter what discipline it is. It is a topic tailor-made: science and social studies integrated for a common purpose—to save the earth. I love it!

We start with the science side of environmental learning. Working with local Indian hatcheries, my students raise fertilized coho salmon eggs. They care for the salmon as the fish develop from egg to fry to fingerling. They keep charts on water temperature, take daily tests for pH, change the water, clean the tank, and watch their salmon grow. They solve problems like what to do when power goes out during a storm or when the refrigeration unit stops working. The students examine the eggs with microscopes, make little books about the development of the salmon egg, and trace the life cycle of the salmon from stream bed to the Pacific Ocean and back. They know what salmon need for survival, and they can list the problems salmon are having in the

Northwest. Early on we integrate the science of salmon, first with language arts and then with social studies. As my knowledge and experience with salmon raising increase, I am able to see more connections and that we are raising not only fish but also ten-year-olds' awareness of the plight of salmon and the widespread ramifications of this local issue.

We are the first class to raise salmon on our island and we want to share our knowledge and our fish with others. The students decide to write one-page plays about the problems (see pages 188–189 in the appendix for a detailed plan) and create the Sockeye Salmon Theater using my husband's widowed athletic socks. They give their plays to most of the classes in the school so all the students learn about salmon and the concerns related to the salmon's return.

This is a real issue in our area. Salmon are crucial to the economic health of our state. Many families earn their livelihood from the fishing industry, either directly or indirectly. The students are very aware that there is a problem because local broadcasts and newspapers seldom go more than a week without some salmon-related headline. Using the puppet play as a medium to educate others about the problems of salmon is very effective.

The students also create a huge comic book describing the plight

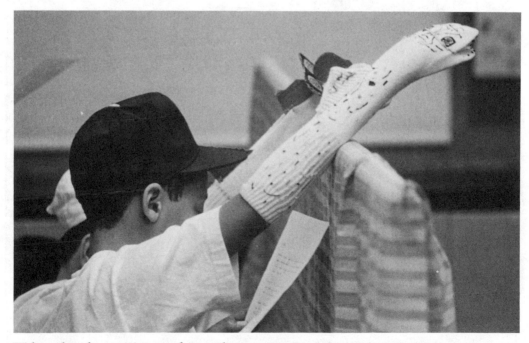

Widowed socks turn into sockeye salmon puppets, as the students create one-page plays to teach others about the plight of salmon.

117

Activating Learning

of the salmon and hang it in the front hall of the school for all to see and learn from. Their book is based on their classroom activities and the information in a similar book prepared by the Department of Fisheries. (Figure 6–1 shows a page from the students' book.)

"The Return of the Salmon Chief"
As the students connect the salmon historically with the Indians of the Northwest Coast by learning about fishing lore and fishing expertise, the American Indian thread reappears in our tapestry of learning. The kids describe different styles of fishing used by the Indians until treaties forced them to stop. They become aware of the historical politicization of the salmon industry, especially in Washington state, when Judge Boldt ruled that the Indians had the power to grant non-Indians fishing rights, not the reverse.

Local Indian lore relates that each year the salmon chief sends a scout to see how things are. If the salmon scout is treated respectfully by the people, he will go back with a positive report and the salmon chief will lead the fish on a return to the rivers and streams. However, if the scout is treated poorly, the salmon will return no more.

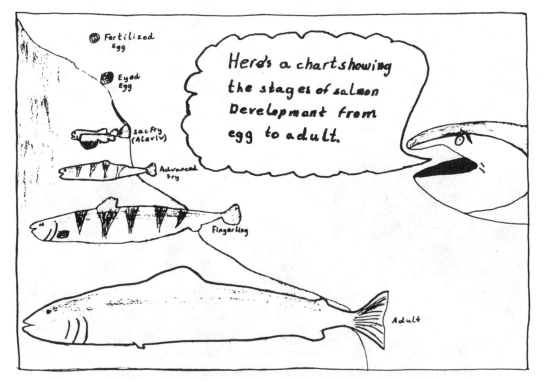

Figure 6–1: Andrew's comic book page helps the whole school learn about salmon.

The pivotal question for students becomes, How can we ensure the return of the salmon chief? They have deduced that if the salmon can no longer return, then the life on this planet is in pretty miserable shape: streams fouled, rivers blocked, oceans overfished, and development unbalanced.

Connecting Through Commercials

We begin looking for answers. First stop, *Fifty Simple Things Kids Can Do to Save the Earth* (Javna 1990). Each student chooses one of the fifty things to share with the rest of us. After discussing these environmental problems in class, we decide to put together some "Saturday Night Live"–type commercials to address them. Each student takes responsibility for one problem. The goal: produce a sixty-second commercial stating the problem and suggesting one thing kids can do about it in an engaging and entertaining way. Some students immediately enlist others to work on their "spot."

Others decide to handle it by themselves. All over the room, different kinds of activities are going on. I hear tunes being hummed, see posters being made, watch faces screw in concentration as text is composed. Another bonbon moment!

I see the need for some limits, however: three boys are now using the length of the room and half the hallway for a river race. "Don't forget, you are going to present these as if they are inside a television set. Let's say that it's a really big-screen TV, about the size of the blackboard. Keep your action within that width and height. Yes, you can bring in costumes. No, you can't throw candy."

After the first dress rehearsal, we discuss problems: some kids talk too fast, some kids don't "stay in character," some kids talk too softly. But overall, it's pretty entertaining and surprisingly effective. We make out a schedule and invite other classes to sign up for when they'd like us to perform "30 Minutes Live to Save the Earth" for them. Notes go home to parents to invite them to drop in. We decide to make a videotape so we can enjoy it and have it available for families who can't come to school during the day.

Conducting Independent Investigations

Working with a friend outside the class or with their families, each student researches an environmental topic independently. They can use any medium or combination of media: poster, essay, debate, video, demonstration, play, poetry. The presentation should take no less than five minutes, no more than seven.

Kevin works on his environmental project using multiple intelligences.

We brainstorm possible topics, ranging from deforestation, the spotted owl controversy, and the taking down of the dams to chlorofluorocarbons, recycling, and the weatherproofing of houses. The assignment is made just before spring break, so there is plenty of time. This is one of the few true "homework" assignments all year. Most often students are simply finishing work at home they didn't complete in class. But I know if we really want to make a difference, it will take more than the good intentions of my students. I want to enlist their families and their friends as we try to make the world a better place.

The results are spectacular. Charts inform about the rain forest, graphs show the growth of the ozone hole, and videos demonstrate the environmentally sound home. Still photographs of a student inside a paper-recycling bin show what other stuff people have thrown into it. A "TV talk show" host interviews experts about saving the earth. Poetry explores the population explosion and the cycle of hunger. Posters list steps to "Save the Salmon Chief." Ecotrivia games and surveys alert us to products people use that harm the environment. The diversity is astonishing. The integrity of the information is impeccable. The presentations range from okay to awesome. The students are very pleased with themselves, deservedly so.

Becoming Community Activists

The students feel impelled to do something for Earth Day so we brainstorm some ideas. The local recycling station is run by a high school environmental club called The Committee to Save the Earth, that helped fund the refrigerator unit for our salmon tank. Now, the club invites us to help them raise our community's consciousness about Earth Day. My students decide to "Picket for the Planet." Bringing in a parent who is in advertising is the first step. She shows the students how to make effective informational placards, helping them see that size, message, and color are all important considerations. After creating placards and mounting them on cedar laths, all the fifth graders march four miles from our school to the local recycling center in the middle of our business district. When they arrive, they are greeted by the mayor and the city manager, who recognize their dedication to the environment. Then the students go to work. Some work at the recycling center. Others take up positions in grocery stores around town, helping with demonstrations about wise consuming, composting, and precycling. Working with secondary students is very powerful. Fifth graders enjoy linking up with older students as well as leading younger ones.

Becoming Environmentally Conscious Entrepreneurs

Our class is buddies with a first-grade class. The fifth graders want to make something that will help their buddies learn, so they create an *A,B,C–1,2,3 Coloring Book to Save the Environment*. It is a series of black felt-tip drawings of beneficial environmental practices, and a single copy costs fifty cents to produce. We borrow fifty dollars from the PTA and print one hundred copies. Giving one to each of our first-grade buddies, we sell out the rest for one dollar at open house. We pay off our debt and finance a second printing, which nearly sells out as well. We make a profit of ninety dollars, which helps another fifth-grade class buy some of the equipment needed to set up their own salmon tank. Culminating learning becomes an economics lesson and a real-life application of citizenship.

Making the American Indian Connection, Again

Reweaving the American Indian thread provides a vehicle for reflection. (Jan Hoem created this very special activity in our first year of integrating.) The students pretend to be an Indian elder. "Recall something from your past, share something from the present, and predict something for the future." In character, wearing the Chilkat blanket we have made in class, each child makes a speech. Tony integrates knowledge and values in his:

> How, my name is Big Hawk, which is my sacred name but the name I go by is Tom Hawkson. I have lived on the great spirits land for one hundred winters and ninety-nine summers.
>
> I remember as a boy climbing many hills and viewing the Great Spirit's land. I saw no skyscrapers. I could breathe the clean air and could see Mt. Rainier, or as we call it Mt. Tahoma, in all its beauty. There were hundreds of trees. It was beautiful. I could see and smell many beautiful flowers. I was able to observe many, many animals building dens or homes and scouting out food. I could see many deer frolicking in the meadows. We had no worries of pollution on the land. I do recall fishing in the river and catching many fish in the wonderful, sparkling-clean, unpolluted water. We had enough in one catch to feed two longhouses full of people. Now we catch very few. Now those that have crossed the land and call themselves Americans have come and taken over. Everywhere I look, the fresh clean air and water have been polluted by machinery, chemicals, waste, and the smoke from big factories. Where I saw hundreds of trees, giant skyscrapers have been built.
>
> I would like all the people to remember we must control what waste we dump in our waters, in our air, and on to our land. We must also control the amount of logging we do and the areas we do the logging. We need to have controls on building skyscrapers. We have to protect our land from pollution and overdevelopment if we want our grandchildren and their children to use and enjoy the land the Great Spirit has given us.

Tapping the Power of the Pen

Active learning also means activism. My students, using their skills in letter writing, write letters to legislators and corporate officers. They learn how to write persuasively and passionately about things that matter to them. For instance, after studying about the effects of the Prince William Sound oil spill, they wrote a letter to one of our senators, supporting a bill for double-hulled tankers.

I always send a copy of each letter that "goes public" home so parents are informed. I once had a parent ask me whether his child would receive a lower grade if she didn't sign one of our public letters.

**Michelle writes a letter
to express her opinion.**

My response? "Of course not." One of the cornerstones of my teaching is respect for individual decisions. Certainly, this class activity honors that respect. That respect has been accomplished when a child does decide not to sign and does so comfortably. More often, though, the letters are individual, personal, and based on solid knowledge. The classic format of a persuasive letter in my room is:

1. Identify the problem.
2. Discuss alternative solutions, including costs and benefits of each.
3. Suggest the best solution and support it with further detail.
4. Be accurate, succinct, and respectful throughout.

MAKING QUICK-AND-QUIET BOOKS

Active learning includes creating learning materials for the class. We frequently create our own books. "Quick-and-quiet books" usually culminate a field trip or are created after we have heard someone speak at our school. I named them that because they capture the essence of some recent class activity quickly and quietly (see pages 190–191 in the appendix for detailed plans.) For example, at the end of our study of immigration, we often take a field trip to the International District in Seattle. While less than thirty minutes away from our school, many children have never visited this unique neighborhood in our metropolitan area. Our suburban island tends to be rather insular and hooked on carpools rather than public transportation. So the first thing we do is use the city bus system to get to the International District. Once there, we spend the day visiting historic sites on a walking tour—the students see the first Chinese school in Seattle and learn how racism kept the International District from being an integrated part of Seattle until quite recently. The students appreciate the outdoor sculptures and visit exhibits at an Asian American museum named in honor of the first Chinese American to become a United States legislator. We eat lunch—six courses!—in a Chinese restaurant at large round tables that seat ten. We invite parents who work downtown to join us. Chopsticks, tiny cups of tea, and fortune cookies highlight the meal. It's one of the few times that we spend an hour over food, talking and sharing the adventures of the day.

After lunch we break up into small groups and explore the tiny shops. Prior to the field trip, we practice appropriate reactions to anything unusual we might see, taste, or smell. The International District is a neighborhood. Pointing, talking loud, making faces or rude noises, just aren't acceptable. We are guests, and we need to be polite and thoughtful. It's a great experience for these ten-year-olds, especially when they visit the herbal medicine shops, peer into the fish markets, cruise the vegetable stalls on the street, or enter the doors of Asian bakeries.

Once we arrive back in the classroom, we capture everything the students can remember in a list. Usually we end up with forty or fifty different things the students recall as interesting or remarkable. Using the lottery box again, each child chooses one thing to record in our book. Using the quick-and-quiet format of picture and short paragraph, the process takes about fifty minutes. (Figure 6–2 is Andy's entry, on locks.) We collect all the pages and bind them into a book. Sometimes we read the book out loud. Sometimes we set up a checkout system so students can take it home. Sometimes we just leave it the classroom for reading workshop.

The quick-and-quiet book can also become a textbook. One year we were really running behind, and it looked like we were going to have to "do" pioneers in a week or not at all. So I asked the students, What's everything you ever wanted to know about pioneers? We listed all the questions on the board. Then we classified the questions by categories: hunting, wagon trains, homesteading, trails, etc. Some of the questions grouped easily under larger topics, some remained highly specific. Back to the lottery box. Each child chose one question to answer. Using the quick-and-quiet format—picture and short paragraph—each child researched and found an answer to the question. In two days, all the questions were answered, and the pages were

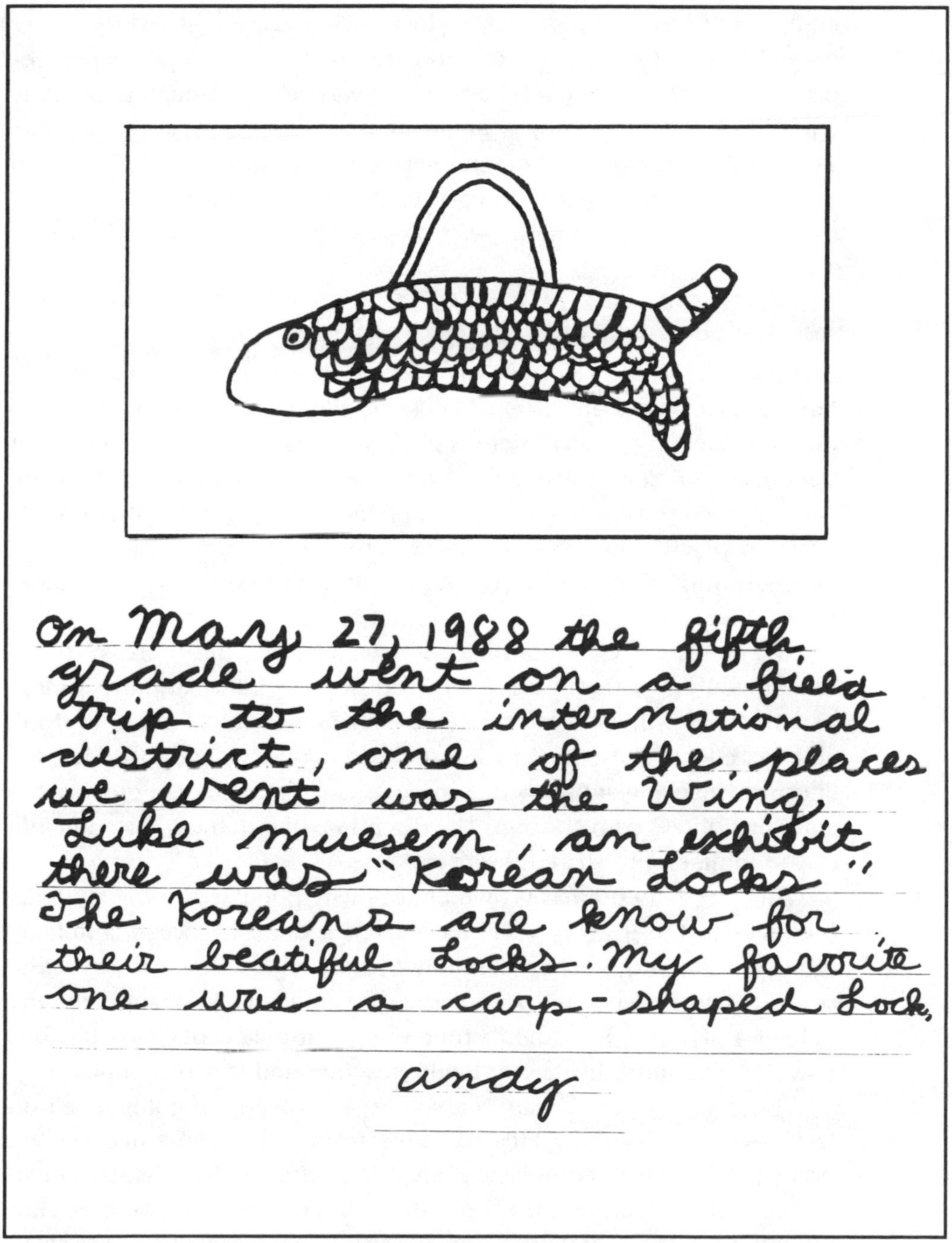

On May 27, 1988 the fifth
grade went on a field
trip to the international
district, one of the places
we went was the Wing
Luke muesem, an exhibit
there was "Korean Locks."
The Koreans are know for
their beatiful Locks. My favorite
one was a carp-shaped Lock.

andy

Figure 6–2: Andy's summary quickly and quietly captures one piece of a terrific field trip.

complete. I ran copies of each child's work and we collated the pages into a book that became our textbook for the final two days of a pioneer preview. The kids loved it. Their writing was valued enough to become a textbook. Their research really needed to be accurate and authentic. Their drawings extended comprehension. It all mattered. It wasn't an onerous task dragging us all down by its sheer weight. Putting the children in charge of their learning was not only quick and quiet but effective.

CREATING A WAX MUSEUM

As I think back, the year we started doing quick-and-quiet books must have been a year of the talkers. Quick-and-quiet books kept the students engaged for forty or fifty minutes in drawing and writing and thus kept talking at a minimum. About that same time, I devised the wax museum activity. (See pages 192–193 in the appendix for a detailed plan.) While I would place it in the category of active learning now, I know my original motivation was more self-serving. I wanted moments of quiet in my classroom.

The more my classroom uses whole learning, the more verbal it becomes: I know that learners need to process information and ideas verbally. I also think learners need to have moments of quiet, to think and to reflect. They need to internalize knowledge and attitudes. So, another balancing act I practice these days is that between quiet space and considerate conversation. The discipline of quietness is as valuable as the jubilation of shared discovery.

The wax museum has grown enormously popular and my students look forward to it every year. We started it one Halloween, a holiday we celebrate in our school and one I really enjoy. However, over the years it had degenerated into scruffy costumes at best and crummy behavior at worst. It seemed a time to try out unacceptable behaviors. I was feeling more like a cop than a teacher, and it wasn't much fun.

The wax museum began as a way to keep learning going, even on Halloween. I asked the kids to move from horror into history. We brainstormed a list of historical events. Then the children divided themselves into work groups, the only rule being that no one could be shut out and no one could work alone. Groups as large as eight and as small as two began working, choosing a historical scene to portray. We talked about our audience, which ranged from kindergartners through fifth graders. We talked about what could be kind of Halloweenish but not scary for the little kids, yet interesting enough for our peers. Ideas came one on top of the other, and enthusiasm built at an exponential rate.

Students created backdrops and props out of butcher paper and cardboard. They collected clothing from home or borrowed from each other to complete their costumes. By Halloween morning each scene was set.

Here's how it works. Other classes in our school begin their Halloween observation with a visit to our classroom. We turn off all the lights and draw all the shades. Each scene is lit by a string of Christmas lights. The room takes on a pleasantly altered state, shadowy and very unschool-like.

"Knock, knock, knock." The children stop talking and check their positions in their tableaus. Each one is aware how much it means to stay in character—laughing, moving, taking the focus, will ruin the entire scene for everyone, spectator and actor alike. The door swings open and in troops a class. A hush falls over the visitors as they walk quietly around the room, viewing each scene, whispering behind their hands. The scenes are perfect—no one moves, no one blinks. I think some of the children even forget to breathe. In less than three minutes, that class is out the door. Everyone collapses! Chatter, giggles, and jiggles to work out the kinks from standing in one place so long and so still. "Knock, knock, knock." It's another class. Ready? "Welcome to the wax museum."

By three o'clock, every class in school has been by. My students are exhausted. All they want is a cup of cider, a doughnut, and permission to go home. Over their Halloween treats, they comment on what hard work it was, they recall individual student reactions, and they exude a sense of pride in a job well done.

REFLECTIONS

One of the nicest things about being a "seasoned" teacher is that I've lived long enough to collect and create a wide range of lesson strategies and student activities. I can remember when there were basically two kinds of activities in the classroom, workbooks and art projects. And neither one of them had anything to do with what else happened to be going on in the room.

Those days are gone. Now I collect and create activities because they are age appropriate, further understanding, apply a skill, stimulate thinking, or appeal to one of the intelligences. I don't use all the activities I mentioned in this chapter every year. I choose from these and others to provide a rich and varied learning environment as well as to meet the needs of my kids.

I am careful to evaluate an activity or a strategy each time before I use it. Does it really fit this moment in time? Will it move us forward? Is it engaging? Will it be worth the time, energy, and resources needed? What is good for one class may not be particularly helpful to another. No two years are the same, yet each year is familiar and similar. Making choices, solving problems, creating new things, applying tested activities, and using successful strategies make teaching fun and learning active.

Chapter Seven

MAKING TEACHING AND LEARNING CHALLENGING

SOCIAL STUDIES TEACHING AND LEARNING
IS POWERFUL WHEN IT IS CHALLENGING.

—NCSS's *Vision*

Two features make social studies a unique school subject. The first is the diversity of disciplines it comprises. Anthropology, archeology, economics, geography, history, law, philosophy, political science, psychology, religion, and sociology are integral social studies disciplines. The second unique feature is that it brings the controversial and ethical dimensions of a topic to the students' attention. Students need to examine social policy and weigh their decisions in the light of it. It is this challenge to deal with public as well as personal dilemmas, that promotes social understanding and civic efficacy (NCSS 1993, 214).

The instructional strategies we choose can promote seriousness of purpose and thoughtful inquiry, or they can trivialize learning. I find that as my skill, understanding, and knowledge of the issues in social studies grow, the substance of the study in my classroom deepens. I no longer use single-sided activities, ones that expose students to only one point of view or one learning orientation. It is the multidimensional nature of social studies teaching and learning that makes it both exciting and interesting. Students work independently, but also in groups. Interacting with people as well as with ideas and issues is an important part of social studies. I believe the reason some teachers and students don't enjoy social studies is they have only experienced it in one dimension, the open-the-book, read-the-chapter, answer-the-questions dimension.

THINKING CREATIVELY, CRITICALLY, PRODUCTIVELY

I knew something was missing in my early teaching. Then educational researchers began to identify and define higher-order thinking. It made sense. I began to monitor my teaching to see where I could eliminate "monothinking" and find opportunities to challenge all students intellectually. I was appalled when courses, packages, books, and curriculums began to advocate teaching higher-order thinking skills in isolation. I found myself in workshops that demonstrated how to move children through levels of thinking skills for the sake of the levels, not the content: what they were thinking about didn't seem important. Why not, I wondered, think about the content that fifth graders needed to know? Couldn't we incorporate higher-order thinking skills into social studies? So, armed with new pedagogy, I examined my own teaching for ways to expand the learning spectrum in my classroom.

I discovered that teaching from multiple perspectives facilitates higher-order thinking. Studying an issue from different points of view raises questions requiring thoughtful examination. Students can't simply retrieve an answer from their memory bank. They must shift focus and generate alternative solutions.

ENSURING EQUAL ACCESS

I also found I needed to look carefully at my teaching style to ensure all students were getting an equal opportunity to practice higher-order thinking skills. Teachers are basically kind, caring people. In our efforts not to embarrass a child, put him or her on the spot, we may unintentionally exclude that child from higher-level intellectual practice. For instance, in my teaching I noticed that I tended to call on the children I perceived as less capable (for whatever reason) less often when probing for higher-level thinking responses. I was ashamed and embarrassed. How could a child ever learn to think in more complex patterns if never given any opportunity to practice? If kids sense they don't have an equal opportunity to become valued members of the classroom community, it doesn't matter how challenging teaching and learning are.

Fortunately, there are actions we can take to foster positive perceptions. For example, if I let a longer period of time elapse between my question and my call for a response, the answer becomes more thoughtful. There are solid data showing that different ethnic groups have different "wait" times between hearing a question and offering a response. Shy children often need more time as well. A friend of mine asks, "Do you want me to go on to someone else and come back to you later?" Her technique works with ESL students as well. Most researchers agree that we should allow at least five seconds between a question and the call for a response.

We can also make it a point to be aware of the number of times each child has an opportunity to respond during the day, what levels of questions she or he responds to, and the quality of that response. Is the student answering a question that requires her to connect ideas, reason, and evaluate? Is he retrieving a single right answer from a limited number of choices? What about prompts? Do we encourage every child with positive comments or only some? "Gena, I know you've got the answer on the tip of your tongue. I'll give you a little more time."

Acknowledging a child's response with a smile, a comment, or a pat on the shoulder validates that child's contribution. Do we distribute those acknowledgments equitably? If you received consistent, positive acknowledgment of your participation in class, wouldn't you find it rewarding? Wouldn't you like to continue that positive cycle of response, acknowledgement, response, acknowledgment?

Where the action happens in the classroom and the teacher's position within it influences student learning as well. Proximity to the teacher empowers learners. My classroom is an ever-changing kaleidoscope of desks. My students frequently rearrange their seating, and I'm almost always up and moving among them.

Other factors, such as whether and how we touch them and whether and how we reprove them, influence how our students learn. If we want to promote challenging teaching and learning, we need to be aware of the effects of our interactions with our students.

WRITING IN ANOTHER'S SHOES

Looking at events and comprehending issues from a historical perspective is challenging for most intermediate-grade students. The historical novel *Elizabeth Blackwell, First Woman Doctor,* by Rachel Baker (1944), is a hard book to read, but I think the challenge is reasonable. I also ask that as they read, the students keep a journal as if they are Elizabeth, capturing each chapter in an entry that reflects what Elizabeth knows, does, and feels. (See page 194 in the appendix for a detailed plan.) I suggest that since Elizabeth is obviously a very smart and very determined person, she is probably going to make her entries meaty and full rather than trivial. I challenge the students to fool me, to make me think it is really Elizabeth writing. Aaron, who's always been the master of few words, turns in the following:

MY JOURNAL BY ELIZABETH BLACKWELL THROUGH THE EYES OF AARON KARLEN

Chapter 1
I just found out that we are moving to America. Last night there was a fire in the sugar house. Everything was destroyed. Some men offered Dad a loan, but he turned it down and said, "I have decided to emigrate to America with my family." We began packing and waiting. The poor Irish immigrants who came each Spring had been struck by Cholera so when 4 days had passed and no new cases had been reported, we set off.

Chapter 2
Father died. I always spend time at the Stowe's home. Our new home is a lot smaller than our old home back in England. My sisters took me to a public debate at Town Hall. The issue was woman's rights. One man said "A woman's career was only in the kitchen." I did not like that. It was against my father's way of thinking. I got my first taste of what I want to grow up to be. I want to be a physician!

Chapter 3
I take the Packet to Philadelphia because it is the cheapest way. I get seasick along the way. I like Dr. Elder very much. I asked Dr. Jackson if I could be a student in his school. He said there never had been a female doctor before in the U.S.A. I was really, really discouraged when Dr. Jackson said he was unable to help me. Many schools had turned me down. I am very sad. On the twenty-seventh of October, a letter and document came. It said they would let me in!

His model is so marvelous I want all the students to hear what a peer has created. We talk about the strength of his writing, the vocabulary he chooses, and how he stays in character. We discuss what we know about travel and attitudes toward women during this period in history. We look at what was going on in other parts of the world, what discoveries were being made and what other issues were important to the day. Reading, and reflecting on that reading, is important in my classroom. Whether the students are entering their reactions in a personal response journal, discussing their reflections with peers in small groups, or assuming a character's perspective, the time taken is more than compensated for by the depth of learning fostered.

SETTING GOALS

New Year's is a great time to talk about resolutions. My students set personal goals using a Daruma, a Japanese folk doll that is a symbol of patience and perseverance. (See pages 195–196 in the appendix for a detailed plan and model.) The custom is to paint in one eye of the doll when you set your goal, then paint in the other eye when the goal is accomplished.

Setting personal goals focuses responsibility for learning on the child. The kids determine what is important and valuable to them, and together we work to achieve these goals. Helping students achieve competence in something they feel is important reinforces the reality that children are the center of the classroom.

LEARNING THROUGH THE LAW

Some teaching strategies promote critical thinking and civic understanding better than others. A number of law-related strategies offer challenging learning. Mock trials and mock hearings, debates, hypothetical

It must be early in the year: the Darumas have only one eye filled in.

situations, and case studies all appeal to the intellect of the intermediate-grade student. Law-related education tends to deal with substantive issues. It is from real life. It promotes thoughtful participation, frequently challenging students to think on their feet and present reasoned arguments before an audience.

Finding an Issue

Imagine this. We have released our salmon into a local stream. We have practiced thinking on many different levels using real content. The time is right to focus on an issue of concern in our region.

In the 1920s a canal was cut from Lake Union in Seattle into Puget Sound. Locks were put in to facilitate boat traffic, accommodating businesses in Lake Union. The canal was cut where there had been a small river, a river by which steelhead and coho salmon traveled to and from their spawning beds, so "fish ladders" were constructed to accommodate them. Then, in 1972, Congress passed the Marine Mammals Protection Act forbidding the killing of any marine mammals. By 1987, sea lions were becoming a nuisance in many places up and down the Pacific Coast. One group of sea lions moved into the entrance of the locks, gobbling up the returning salmon like pigs at a banquet. State fisheries agents became increasingly concerned as the sea lions feasted on greater and greater numbers of the fish and the fish runs became smaller and smaller. Scientists therefore began experimenting with ways to divert or remove the sea lions.

One sea lion in particular, dubbed Herschel, caught the fancy of the reporters and their readers. Evening telecasts featured the big, brown-eyed mammal. Newspapers carried him on their front pages. Herschel and his buddies foiled many different schemes to rid the locks of the sea lion. Vile-tasting condiments, rubber-tipped arrows, and underwater noise did not deter them. Marine biologists even trucked Herschel and his buddies down to California. It took only fifteen days for the "boys" to make it back to the locks, hungrier than ever. It looked like federal law was going to protect one species, which was abundant, to the annihilation of another, which was becoming increasingly rare.

This story is an example of the kind of regional issue that can capture intermediate-grade students' intellectual attention. I decided to use this real-life scenario for a mock trial (Armancas-Fisher, Gold, and Lindquist 1991). My students had never staged a trial before, but this material seemed tailor-made: it involved current issues and two distinct, appealing players, the steelhead salmon and the sea lion. It was a real dilemma with no single solution. It would require research into state and federal laws, like the Marine Mammal Act. Several concerned groups formed themselves into some surprising alliances: American Indian groups, sports fishermen, and commercial fishermen sided with the State Department of Fisheries to force Herschel and his buddies out, dead or alive. Greenpeace, federal agents, and ecologically concerned citizens formed an opposition group that insisted the Marine Mammal Act should not be revised or amended in any way. The trial simulation wrapped many of the separate threads we had been studying throughout the year into a single, cohesive pattern.

Preparing for the Trial
Mock trials are interesting intellectual exercises. Everyone, child or adult, is excited by courtroom drama. In the process of planning the defense or prosecution, students encounter higher-level thinking skills at every turn. They must analyze the evidence, synthesize arguments, propose suppositions in the form of questions, and develop well-reasoned arguments. The students acting as jurors must come to a decision that is defensible. Additionally, the students learn how a trial really works, which is a far cry from the *Perry Mason*–style TV trial. I invite lawyers, law students, or judges into my classroom to help the students develop their cases. I don't know that much about trials, but there are a lot of people who do and who are pleased to be asked to come into the classroom for an hour to work with students.

The students have to work cooperatively in groups during a mock trial. I've found it is important not to assign specific roles until the last minute: having teams work on prosecution and defense strategies rather than immediately assigning three students to be prosecutors and three others to be defense attorneys keeps the whole class more involved. Assigning two people to every witness role so they can practice their testimony in pairs also increases interest and enhances preparation.

We begin by researching salmon-industry and endangered-species issues. Using the Lexus computer network, I select newspaper articles from the *Los Angeles Times*, the *Seattle Times*, and *The Washington Post*. Each article highlights a different point of view and reveals important information. The students read the articles in small groups and identify the facts that support the sea lion and the facts that support the steelhead.

While developing their understanding of the issue, the students also become familiar with procedural justice, in other words, "due process." We recall our study of the Constitution and the Bill of Rights, other threads of justice and law that weave in and out of our year's work.

Kevin researches data for his team's trial presentation.

Next, the class investigates trial procedures. They identify the major steps in a trial and the parties to civil and criminal cases. (See pages 197–198 in the appendix for a detailed breakdown of trial steps.) At this point, a lawyer speaks to the class about the concept of "innocent until proven guilty beyond a reasonable doubt." Then, using stipulated facts and witness depositions, the students complete a time line of relevant events.

Now come the most challenging activities. First the students describe the main arguments in favor of each side. Then they identify the facts that support or weaken each major argument. Finally, they write an opening argument for each side.

Armed with all this information, the students compose possible questions for direct and cross-examinations. The witnesses rehearse their stories, being sure they stay within the facts of the sworn statements.

The day before the trial, a lawyer friend comes in to preside over a rehearsal. The alternates play the roles, and the others watch and learn.

Presenting the Trial

On the day of the trial, the students dress up, looking as professional as ten-year-olds can. Some carry briefcases. The boys wear sports coats and ties. The girls pull their hair back and wear colored tights under their good dresses. Some parents attend, and we invite the other fifth-grade classes. A photographer shows up from the local paper. Herschel the Sea Lion is tried for the murder of Sam Steelhead at the Ballard Locks.

While the jury deliberates, the judge, a Washington State Supreme Court Justice, debriefs the attorneys and the witnesses, commenting on the strength of their cases, things they might have added, and how this mock trial differed from an actual one. She explains her rulings on objections and discusses the effectiveness of their strategies. Finally, the jury files in: guilty!

Considering Alternatives

We hold a final debriefing as a class. We analyze the weak and strong points of each case as it was presented. Then we evaluate the trial from the standpoint of its success in achieving justice. Finally we ask, Could we have accomplished this in a different way?

I don't want children to leave this activity thinking that litigation is the only way or the best way to solve a problem. Certainly our yearlong commitment to mediation cannot be abandoned, either in the classroom or in the community. The children need to know arbitration is also an avenue for solving differences. While mock trials are very engaging, I use them sparingly. They tend to foster divisiveness, a win-lose mentality I work hard to move children away from.

We revisit the problem using mediation or arbitration so the children experience different options and have an opportunity to verbalize what they feel, know, and do as they compare multiple ways we can use to solve problems.

CONTROVERSIAL ISSUES IN THE CLASSROOM

Teaching and learning are challenging in a classroom in which controversial issues are examined. How do we study these issues without letting our own biases and values blocking independent, thoughtful critiques by our students? Here are some steps that work for me:

◆ *Expose* students to sources of information that include diverse perspectives, and offer conflicting opinions.

- *Teach* students how to present a point of view in a reasoned manner. Practice using language associated with reasonableness: *from my point of view, one consideration, some people feel, my personal opinion is, based on evidence from.*
- *Provide models* for examining content thoughtfully and with seriousness of purpose. I frequently invite lawyers and judges into my classroom and ask them to tell us how they go about thinking about an issue. I urge them to give us samples of their thinking, examples of the way they phrase their thoughts. At first the students mimic the models. Later, the habits of thoughtful speaking find their way into the children's speech.
- *Weigh* costs and benefits. We used to talk about pros and cons, but in our increasingly complex world issues are seldom so clearly defined. Instead, most issues fall somewhere in between, depending on one's point of view. Solutions to most issues are multiple. The choice frequently depends on the perception of balance between the costs and the benefits.
- *Share* information on student decisions without creating a win-lose mentality. Conducting opinion polls, placing choices along a continuum, and writing editorials are all strategies that encourage students to make decisions in a reasoned, thoughtful manner rather than on what their best friend thinks.

DEAR EDITOR

Writing editorials or letters to the editor is a worthwhile, challenging activity for intermediate-grade learners as a unit of study draws to a close. Letters to the editor can be mailed; editorials can be published in the classroom. Preparing opinions for print encourages careful as well as thoughtful writing.

Sometimes we publish a "What I Think" paper, collecting everyone's ideas into one culminating statement. Like letters to the editor, these papers identify the problem, look at alternative solutions, choose one, and give reasons for that choice.

Why make believe when there is a real audience out there? Real writing is what we want these students to do when they grow up, so let's start now. Real writing has an immediacy to it, and a real-world application shouldn't be missed. Mailing a child's letter, whether to the local newspaper, a children's magazine, or a television program, authenticates it. We collect a list of "People to Write To," placing names and addresses on a chart hanging in the back of the room. Students have wide choices for making their writing real.

The following letter was written by Matt at the conclusion of study the class made of old-growth forests and the spotted owl controversy. The students researched different points of view and simulated a Senate hearing. Some students role-played legislators, whose responsibility it was to make a decision regarding this intensely emotional local issue, while others represented various community groups with a vested interest in the outcome.

> Lakeridge Elementary School
> 8215 SE 78th
> Mercer Island, WA 98040
>
> Editor
> The Seattle Times
> P. O. Box 70
> Seattle, WA 98111
>
> Dear Editor,
>
> I am in the fifth grade and have been studying the spotted owl controversy. The owls should be protected as should the old growth forests. The logging industry has been too caught up in cutting down as many trees as possible in order to make a profit. Because of this, they have not done a good job replacing the trees. The logging industry is going to go out of business sooner or later if they keep clear-cutting. We should stop now and save many trees.
>
> We should start by training some of the loggers for other jobs. The minimum number of loggers should be left, so we can cut the fewest trees needed to provide products such as paper, pencils, etc. The loggers should have to replace what they cut with a variety of different trees. Also, effort should be put into trying to replace wood with another substance whenever possible, so that fewer trees will have to be destroyed. In the future, we should ban clear-cutting completely. Only cutting little sections of the forest should be allowed. From my point of view, that would be the best way to do things.
>
> > Sincerely,
> > Matt

LEARNING THROUGH COMMUNITY SERVICE

Engaging in community service combines hands-on, heads-on, and hearts-on learning in an especially effective way. "Integrating service to the community intentionally with curricular content . . . has proven to be a more effective and long-lasting educational method than classroom instruction alone" (Armancas-Fisher, Gold, and McPherson 1992, 2).

Community service provides challenging learning because students need to:

1. Identify a problem.
2. Choose a solution.
3. Devise a plan of action.
4. Organize and carry out the plan.
5. Evaluate the results.

The types of projects students in the intermediate grades can successfully carry out are many and varied: adopting and cleaning up a local stream, tutoring younger children, recycling school wastepaper, conducting a food drive as part of a study on hunger. Participating in community service grounds learning in real-life connections and challenges.

HEARING FROM THE EXPERTS

Teaching and learning in the social studies lend themselves to bringing outside experts into the classroom. The expert may be a renowned practitioner in a particular field, a parent or a neighbor who knows about something special that fits into a current focus of study, or a community service agent who has a special point of view.

While inviting the expert has long been a teacher function, in the child-centered classroom the students select the topic, contact the speaker, arrange the schedule, and follow up with a thank-you note.

Expertise can be developed within the classroom as well. Students can be challenged to obtain and share expertise in selected topics that will enrich and extend the knowledge of the whole class. In my classroom, this expertise is usually acquired through research and shared through an oral presentation. Plenty of resources, plenty of time, and a clearly understood goal are essential; models or prototypes are helpful.

Remember, though: don't have twenty-eight experts give twenty-eight oral reports one right after the other. If your goal is to enlarge and enrich the class's understanding, awareness, and appreciation, back-to-back presentations by each member of the class guarantees defeat. Your rule of thumb: divide them up. Never plan more than four or five

Erica knows becoming a classroom expert takes resources, time, and work.

presentations a day. Start the morning off with one session. Change focus, and do something that involves the whole body or a different kind of skill. Have another session after morning recess. Take time prior to lunch for a third session. After lunch, work in a fourth session. Midafternoon, present a fifth. If needed, have a final session before school is dismissed.

Here are additional suggestions for keeping interest alive:

1. *Change the ambience*. Have a gallery opening, with refreshments catered by the presenters. Set up a scientific convention, or pattern the presentations on popular television formats (*Meet the Press*, *Crossfire*, *Oprah Winfrey*, or *People's Court*).

2. *Expect the listeners to interact with the student experts*. Sometimes one third of my students are responsible for presenting, one third are responsible for writing newspaper reviews of the presentations, and one third act as a participatory audience. Each student in the audience is expected to ask at least one question during a question-and-answer session. The students rotate roles, so that in three days

141

each of the students has experienced all three kinds of interaction.

3. *Expect the experts to use more than one style of informing the audience.* Charts, music, movement, and pictures are all part of well-rounded presentations. Expecting student experts to add these components to their oral presentations challenges them to be creative as well as accurate. Their information will be more memorable to the classroom audience as the multiple intelligences are tapped.

4. *Give students an opportunity to practice.* Split the class up into several small support groups of four or five students. Ask them to listen to and critique one another's presentations. Any information the students hear more than once has a greater likelihood of being remembered later.

5. *Collect and publish the products of the presentations.* Charts, graphs, key words, steps in a process, or pictures can be captured for reviewing and reliving. Classroom newspapers, videos, booklets, bulletin boards, or classroom displays are some ways we like to publish.

EMBRACING TECHNOLOGY

Increasingly sophisticated instructional tools and data resources are available for use in our classrooms. I find it challenging to keep up with and integrate the latest technology. Electronic mail, computerized databases and other software programs, laser disks, hypermedia, and scanners have the potential to influence my teaching and my students' learning profoundly. My students have discovered that video reports are challenging to conceive and carry out. They find that incorporating visual images can make their message more powerful than when conveyed through words alone.

Few studies have been done to investigate the best application of these innovations. We'll have to experiment ourselves, weighing costs and benefits. Moving the application into higher-level thinking, not creating a room full of data jockeys, is the trick. Simply using a modem to talk to a student somewhere else in the world does not make a superior social studies program. It is what the students talk about that matters. Playing "Oregon Trail" does not make a technologically savvy social studies program. Probing the reasoning behind real rather than random choices creates critical thinking. Pulling isolated facts from a computer encyclopedia does not create facile writers who communicate with integrity and passion. Helping students use technology effectively and managing multiple resources are new roles for teachers (NCSS 1993, 222).

REFLECTIONS

Challenging teaching and learning come in many forms. They are communicated by how we teach as well as what we teach. They are fostered through a variety of experiences that tap into different kinds of knowing and doing. One of our roles as teachers is to make sure our students' thinking is stimulated and challenged through the multidimensional qualities of social studies. We must also communicate to our students the value of careful work, thoughtful comments, and critical thinking. Our reactions to student thinking are a way to communicate these values. By not accepting a student answer at face value but probing for the reasoning behind the answer, we set a higher standard for thinking. Challenging student assumptions sensitively, in a trusted relationship, encourages intellectual growth and development. In the intermediate grades, we can habitually require our students to explain their answers, asking them to use content as the basis for their reasoning. "Just because" no longer is an acceptable response.

It has been my experience that learning students consider challenging they also view as worthwhile. Simulations, real-world connections, and projects involving the multiple intelligences challenge students and teachers to solve problems creatively and to share their solutions. Challenging learning and teaching combine the hands, the head, and the heart so that doing and knowing matter, so that learning makes a difference.

Chapter Eight

ACCENTING ASSESSMENT

I PROMISE YOU EVERY DAY YOUR CHILDREN
WILL LEARN SOMETHING. SOME DAYS
THEY'LL BRING IT HOME IN THEIR HANDS.
SOME DAYS THEY'LL BRING IT HOME IN
THEIR HEADS. AND SOME DAYS THEY'LL
BRING IT HOME IN THEIR HEARTS.
                    —Valerie Welk

Three times a year I have to "give grades." It's not my favorite thing to do. In a classroom where whole learning is taking place, grades have little relevance. No one in my classroom fails. Fortunately, a new language is developing in the profession, a language of assessment that has little or nothing to do with grades. I wish that were true of the school district I teach in: I still have to give grades three times a year.

I frequently question the purpose of the whole process of grading when I am staring at the first of twenty-eight report cards to be filled out. However, I am always pleasantly surprised at what I learn about my teaching when I focus on where all the children are at a particular point in time. Giving grades does help me spot weak areas in my teaching. It helps me identify concepts and skills that need further practice. It reminds me of the developmental level of my students.

I don't use grades daily in my classroom: it's a waste of time. If I graded every single piece of work we produce, we'd do much less. The students would have less practice and less-varied experiences. The application and synthesis of knowledge and attitudes are ongoing, ever-improving activities. Why should we grade each little step in our students' widening sphere of accomplishment? Learning something new is like throwing a pebble in a pond. A first small circle of understanding appears when the pebble hits the water. Successive practice expands learning and broadens the circles of knowledge. I don't think we need to grade every ripple. Why not, instead, provide more practice for multiple kinds of intelligences and different learning styles?

I find many students look at a grade as an end product. They don't interpret it as "becoming" or "growing" or "developing." Neither do many of their parents. They read it as "This is IT!" Frequently the grade becomes the attitude—"I got a C in geography, but that's okay because I don't like it much anyway." When that child grows up to be a parent, teachers hear, "Oh, I wasn't good in geography either. That's why Johnny doesn't do well."

As I move deeper into whole learning, I have discovered grading simply doesn't communicate the process of learning I value. A's, B's, and C's or 1's, 2's, and 3's have little to do with monitoring the daily effectiveness and quality of student participation in lessons and activities. After teaching a split fourth/fifth-grade class for a couple of years and having half the class as fourth graders one year and fifth graders the next, I've also discovered that one school year is not really enough time to determine what a child has learned or what I have taught. I noticed, for instance, that skills the fourth graders were not able to produce consistently in June were fully mastered when they walked in the door in September to begin fifth grade. Something good must have happened over the summer!

I wish we could look at learning from kindergarten through fifth or sixth grade as one continuum instead of trying to parse it up into finite bits for evaluation. Learning is truly cumulative at this age. Learning is like weaving, sometimes the same threads are used in the same pattern, sometimes the same threads are used in a new pattern. Sometimes new threads are used, combining with the familiar threads to deepen an existing pattern or to create a new one. One day, from the myriad of threads a beautiful holistic pattern emerges. Knowing emerges at different times for different children. Each pattern is individual and unique. Each worthy and valuable. Perhaps that's what we should really be evaluating.

ASSESSMENT FOR MULTIPLE INTELLIGENCES

In *Teaching and Learning Through the Multiple Intelligences* (1992), Campbell, Campbell, and Dickinson differentiate between assessing the intelligences directly and how to assess *through* the intelligences (199–200). The more I think about it, the more I find assessment needs to be "multiplied" into diverse forms so that children have several options for demonstrating what they know, can do, or feel.

**Julie designs a brochure
to show what she knows.**

The notion of multiple ways to assess reforms the traditional idea of grading. As I experiment with assessment in my classroom, I find each year it becomes more individual, more child centered. The Campbells and Dickinson suggest "menus" as a way to infuse variety into classroom assessment (203–5). Drawing from their lists, I've fashioned a menu for the social studies–integrated classroom that draws from multiple intelligences. These options could be used as a goal for all the students to sample during a school year:

LINGUISTIC

Use storytelling to explain—

Write journal entries on—

Write a letter to—

LOGICAL/MATHEMATICAL

Create a time line of—

Make a strategy game that includes—

Select and use technology to—

KINESTHETIC

Build or construct a—

Role-play or simulate—Kinesthetic

Design a model for—

VISUAL/SPATIAL

Chart, map, cluster, graph—

Use a memory system to learn—Visual/Spatial

Design a poster, bulletin board, mural of—

MUSICAL

Write song lyrics for—

Collect and present songs about—

Write a new ending to a song or musical composition so that it explains—

INTERPERSONAL

Identify and assume a role to—

Use a conflict management strategy to—Interpersonal

Help resolve a local or global problem by—

INTRAPERSONAL

Set a goal to accomplish—

Describe how you feel about—Intrapersonal

Write a journal entry on—

This kind of assessment is exciting for both teacher and students, because the students own the whole process from beginning to end, and it's natural, not forced. No one has to fit a single mold. No one has to demonstrate knowing, doing, and feeling in a single "right" way.

TEST THE TEACHER

I don't test a lot, but when I do, it is mainly to give students practice in taking tests. I happen to believe the test tests the teacher. Did I teach what I thought I was teaching? How well? To how many? What do I need to do differently next time? Do I need to find another way to provide practice? What do the students know, what can they do, and how do they feel? What will they remember ten years from now?

It's my job to use instructional strategies that elicit and support the objective of the specific assignment and the overall goals of the year. Since my overall goal is "to help young people develop the ability to make informed and reasoned decisions for the public good as citizens of a culturally diverse, democratic society in an interdependent world" (NCSS 1993, 213), I need to have a large repertoire of activities from which to draw.

OLD SKILLS, NEW APPLICATIONS

Sometimes I think we try too hard to invent new strategies when old familiar strategies are not only comfortable, but still useful. For example, many students, like many of us, need to do something more than once to do it well. That's one reason I use letter writing as a part of assessment all year. I've found using a familiar format, like a friendly letter, encourages intellectual risk taking over time. If the child is always concentrating on the format of an activity rather than the content, that activity does little to further academic application or creative thinking. By repeating a format, many students relax and reveal their knowledge, skills, and attitudes. Balance, of course, is needed to ensure no activity is overworked.

NEW SKILLS, OLD APPLICATIONS

When introducing a new skill to my students, I've often found it helps if we practice the new skill in an old context. For example, when moving from reading time lines to creating time lines from research, setting up the same familiar format and having the students "fill in" the missing information as we discuss the process helps every child practice before applying the new skill independently. Working in pairs or small groups often supports new learning. The notion of "trying on" new skills several times before assessment seems obvious, but sometimes in our hurry-up days, the rehearsal gets lost. Students are often required to jump from introduction to mastery.

Students need to practice. They need to practice again and again over time to maintain and develop concepts and skills introduced early in the learning sequence. This practice need not be exactly the same. Options for extensions and enrichment should be available to keep interest keen. Whole learning gives students time to find appropriate and meaningful ways of integrating information and solving problems across the curriculum.

ALTERNATIVE ASSESSMENT

Alternative assessment is defined as all the ways a student can demonstrate what he or she knows, feels, or can do by any means other than a traditional multiple-choice standardized achievement test (Worthen 1993, 445). I almost always use alternative forms of assessment. Most teachers do; they simply haven't hung new vocabulary on to their methods.

Just like the process of whole learning, alternative assessment should feature the student at the center. I believe part of our responsibility as intermediate-grade teachers is to help students become accurate self-assessors and authentic peer assessors. This is a learning process, just like reading or writing. It takes modeling, discussion, practice, and reflection.

Student-Created Criteria

I save copies of student work from previous years. These models don't have to be the best or the worst. They are the ones kids never get around to taking home or specifically ask me to keep to share "next year." Introducing an activity by holding up a student model I ask, "What is effective about this particular model?" The students discuss what they find effective. I probe, "What could have been done to make it more effective?" and we chat about improvements. I review the points raised, usually writing them on the overhead. When the students begin their own work on the activity, the overhead is left on so they have the "criteria" to refer to easily. Inviting the students to identify and specify criteria in advance promotes higher-quality products.

It is quite easy to take the student criteria and change them into a rubric with a range of points given for each description, category, or quality. Often, the students help determine the "worth" of each description. By the time the students have completed the project, they are very capable of arriving at an authentic assessment of their work. More important, they perceive assessment as an ever-widening circle of competence, rather than a dead-end grade.

Student-created criteria predict what the children hope to accomplish and with what degree of mastery, creativity, and/or cooperation. By setting up the criteria prior to the practice, students have a guide to success in terms they comprehend, because they fashioned the measurements.

Interim Assessment

Remember when Aaron wrote as if he were Elizabeth Blackwell? Before the students began writing their entries, we talked about criteria. What would make our journal entries not just acceptable, but terrific? The students decided the entries had to be believable, accurate, and complete. In this way they predicted, if you will, what success would look like.

After the class had read three chapters and made three subsequent journal entries as Elizabeth, I asked them to exchange journals with a study buddy, a trusted partner chosen by them. The study buddies read the entries against these criteria:

1. Believable? Why or why not?
2. Accurate? Why or why not?
3. Complete? Does it do the job?
4. What is your overall impression?

Sarah, a fifth grader, wrote this assessment to her fourth-grade partner, Aaron:

> Aaron,
>
> While I was reading your delightful entries, I had a smile on my face. The cause of this was your writing. Yes, your writing was so exciting. I could feel your disappointment or your happiness all in your lively sentences.
>
> You got your info. from the book but you wrote the ideas down in a way as if you were Elizabeth looking back at the day's achievements.
>
> I also like the way you opened and closed your entries. The opening was like you wanted to read on and the closing was like you had just finished an exciting adventurous book.
>
> I could go on and on (as I've already started to do) but I will just say, Elizabeth Blackwell is a fabulous writer when she is written through the eyes of Aaron!

In all honesty, if I had read Aaron's finished journal along with twenty-seven others, my assessment comment probably would have been "Good job!" Assessment while an activity is in progress informs the participants. It gives students an opportunity to monitor and adjust, either through their own eyes, the eyes of the teacher, or the eyes of peers.

Peer assessing is powerful. Of course, all children don't respond as Sarah does. So, I asked Sarah's and Aaron's permission to share her assessment. I read it to the class, asking What is effective about this assessment? and we listed the positive attributes. We talked about how it would feel to receive such an assessment. I asked Aaron to describe how he felt when he got it, what he learned from it, and what he planned to do next journal entry.

Postpublication Assessment

Assessment can also take place postpublication. I happen to like having the students use publication as an extension of the assignment. An extension activity often reveals quality—is the journal truly believable, accurate, and complete, for example?

An example of this occurred when the children finished *Elizabeth Blackwell, First Woman Doctor*. We discussed magazine interviews: "Have you ever read one?" Several had. They shared their observations about the form and content of a magazine interview. We discussed the kinds of questions used in interviews and concluded that open-ended ones are more conducive to interesting responses. We spent time brainstorming the kinds of questions we might ask Elizabeth Blackwell if we could interview her for a magazine article. I wrote the questions on the overhead, collecting about fifteen. "Using only your journals, pretend you are a reporter for a magazine and you have the opportunity to interview Elizabeth Blackwell, the first woman doctor. Choose questions from the overhead or make up other ones of your own and interview Elizabeth. You write both the questions for the reporter and the answers for Elizabeth."

I asked the students how many questions they thought would "do the job," and they came to a consensus that seven questions and responses would be enough. Here's Aaron's interview:

> ELIZABETH BLACKWELL WAS THE FIRST WOMAN DOCTOR
>
> *Aaron:* What was the biggest surprise for you in your early years?
>
> *Eliz:* My biggest surprise that I had in my early ages was when my father told my family and I that we were moving to the states [America].

Aaron:	What was your biggest accomplishment in your life?
Eliz:	My biggest accomplishment in my life was opening my hospital.
Aaron:	Why did you never marry?
Eliz:	I never married because men were unfair to women. I didn't want to be ruled by another human being.
Aaron:	Were you ever about to quit being a physician any time in your life? Why or why not?
Eliz:	Sometimes I wanted to quit because of the rough times of riots and injuries.
Aaron:	Why did you decide to adopt a child?
Eliz:	I decided to adopt a child because the child would fill in the missing part in my life. Since I adopted a child I wasn't lonely any more. I had some one to keep me company.
Aaron:	Where did you become a doctor (or learn to be one?)
Eliz:	I learned to be a doctor at La Maternite, a French hospital. I was a nurse there.
Aaron:	Where did you practice?
Eliz:	I practiced in the poor neighborhoods where the people there needed me the most.
Aaron:	What were some of the toughest times you went through in your time being a doctor?
Eliz:	Some of the toughest times that I went through as a doctor were when there were riots and things like that
Aaron:	What did you want to be as a child as a grown up?
Eliz:	I wanted to be a surgeon, but my dreams were totally shattered when I squirted some vaccine in my eye at La Maternite.

Once again, the students handed their work over to their study buddies for peer assessment. Once again the students assessed whether the work was believable, accurate, and complete and summarized their overall impression. Sarah's response to Aaron follows:

Dear Aaron,

It was great how you did [America] in the first answer. That is really what they do for interviews.

This really sounds like an interview with Elizabeth Blackwell. While I was reading it I could see Elizabeth and the journalist talking. This is just how Elizabeth would answer.

You did an excellent job of telling very important facts in an unique way. Maybe next time you might tell a little more. Your writing is superb. You used great words.

Your interview is very well done. It tells the things it needs to tell and leaves out the unimportant things. You need good judgment for this and you sure have it!

Your length is perfect! You did extra work—you have 9 questions! You corrected 99% of your spelling mistakes.

Your sentences are complete along with your entire interview.

If I was grading it I'd give it an A!

I ask my students to do assessment activities all through the year. The procedure just described can easily be a self-assessment instead. However, it can't be a one-shot deal. Children need to learn how to assess their work, they need to learn to identify quality, and they need practice in doing both.

Parents as a Part of the Process

I like to make parents my partners in assessment. Rubrics go home early in an assignment, and parents may choose to read and mark the final draft according to the rubric. When they do, I gain a deeper understanding of their values and their perceptions about their child's capability and success. This parent input becomes part of the matrix when the students and I confer about their work. I read the rough draft in detail, because I learn more about what I need to teach from a rough draft. I don't invite parent input on the rough draft, because many times parent expectations exceed their child's developmental level.

Inviting parent assessment also gives me an opportunity to teach parents about praise and positive comments. I encourage them to balance compliments to criticism two for one. Criticisms sandwiched between compliments work just as effectively for children as for adults. Opening the assessment process to parents increases support for classroom activities.

Self-Assessment

Self-assessment in my classroom is ongoing. Students are constantly asked to reflect on what they have learned, or what they can do, or how they feel. Self-assessment is a good way to culminate an educational field trip: if the child finds the trip worthwhile, the parents realize its value as well, and I know it was worth the time and expense.

I especially like to use self-assessment as a form of immediate feedback when the students are presenting. As an example, let's take an activity in which the students read a biography and then prepare a three-minute oral presentation as if they were the person. They are to use the present tense and at least one appropriate prop. Before the students even select the books they'll read, we develop an assessment sheet for this activity (see Figure 8–1).

After classroom discussion, I suggest they take it home and hang it in an appropriate place when they practice. Then, after the students make their presentations to the class, they mark an assessment sheet and so do I. We compare our opinions and discuss the differences. Almost always, the students are more critical of themselves than I am.

One year we decided to do oral biographies but wanted a new twist. Pretending to be the famous person is fun but we wanted something more. This time, after reading the biographies, we first created storyboards about the subject. The panels of the storyboard were highly structured:

BIOGRAPHY STORYBOARDS

Panel 1–Title.

Panel 2–Main character.

Panel 3–Setting as child or young person.

Panel 4–Situation before becoming famous.

Panel 5–Problems he/she had to overcome.

Panel 6–Greatest accomplishment(s).

Panel 7–Death or what is currently happening in life today.

Panel 8–A six- to ten-sentence paragraph of your feelings about this person. Do you admire him/her? Why or why not? Would this person have been a good friend? Are you inspired because of this person's life? Why or why not?

Then, using tagboard and markers, the students created biography billboards to enhance the oral presentations of the information collected on the storyboard. The students presented their storyboards orally and then responded to questions from the audience. It was fun

ORAL Presentation

1)
Can be heard in the back 1 low ————— wow 5
of room

2) Informative   1 ——+——+——+—— 5

3) Pacing (Not too fast)   1 ——+——+——+—— 5

4) Eye Contact   1 ——+——+——+—— 5

5) Stand Comfortably on 1 ——+——+——+—— 5
   two feet

6) Falls between 3-5 min.
   time limit (5th closer 5min.) 1 ——+——+——+—— 5

7) Comfortable posture, use 1 ——+——+——+—— 5
   natural gestures

8) Use your voice effectively 1 ——+——+——+—— 5

9) Breathe!   1 ——+——+——+—— 5

Optional: props or visuals

Figure 8–1: Oral presentation rubric.

and required them to use their head, hands, and heart in order to complete it. (Daniel's storyboard is shown in Figure 8–2.)

Projects of Excellence

Teachers need to select activities carefully, not draw them at random from a grab bag. The activities we choose must provide the appropriate practice and the measured extensions needed to nudge children along academically and emotionally. I do, however, think we need to culminate and measure learning periodically, establishing benchmarks that reflect how knowledge and skills practiced in the past have been applied to new content.

For example, my students have been writing letters, drawing diagrams, writing newspaper articles, identifying different techniques of persuasion, and designing effective posters. Now, as a benchmark, I assign a "project of excellence" centered on the topic "inventions."

1. Choose an invention you think has had a significant impact on the world. Research it on note cards. Be sure you have all the facts recorded—who, what, where, when, why, and how—so you can share its history.
2. Draw a diagram of your invention, using colors and labels effectively.
3. Prepare a magazine ad to "sell" your invention. Use one of the techniques of persuasion we studied in health.
4. Write a letter to a friend as if you are the inventor the day you got your invention to work. Reveal what you did, what you know, and how you feel.
5. Write a newspaper article as if you are a reporter who has just interviewed the inventor or has just seen the invention working and are breaking the story.
6. Arrange Nos. 2–5 on a piece of 24″ x 36″ poster board, so it can be displayed on the bulletin board.
7. Present your invention at a scientific convention. Use a demonstration to introduce your invention to the group and be prepared to answer questions. Be sure to convince us of its positive impact on the world.

So many pieces of learning are collected in this project! Hands-on, heads-on, hearts-on activities take precedence. The students have to create a product, present information orally, and share values with their peers. The project also requires higher-level thinking: analysis,

157

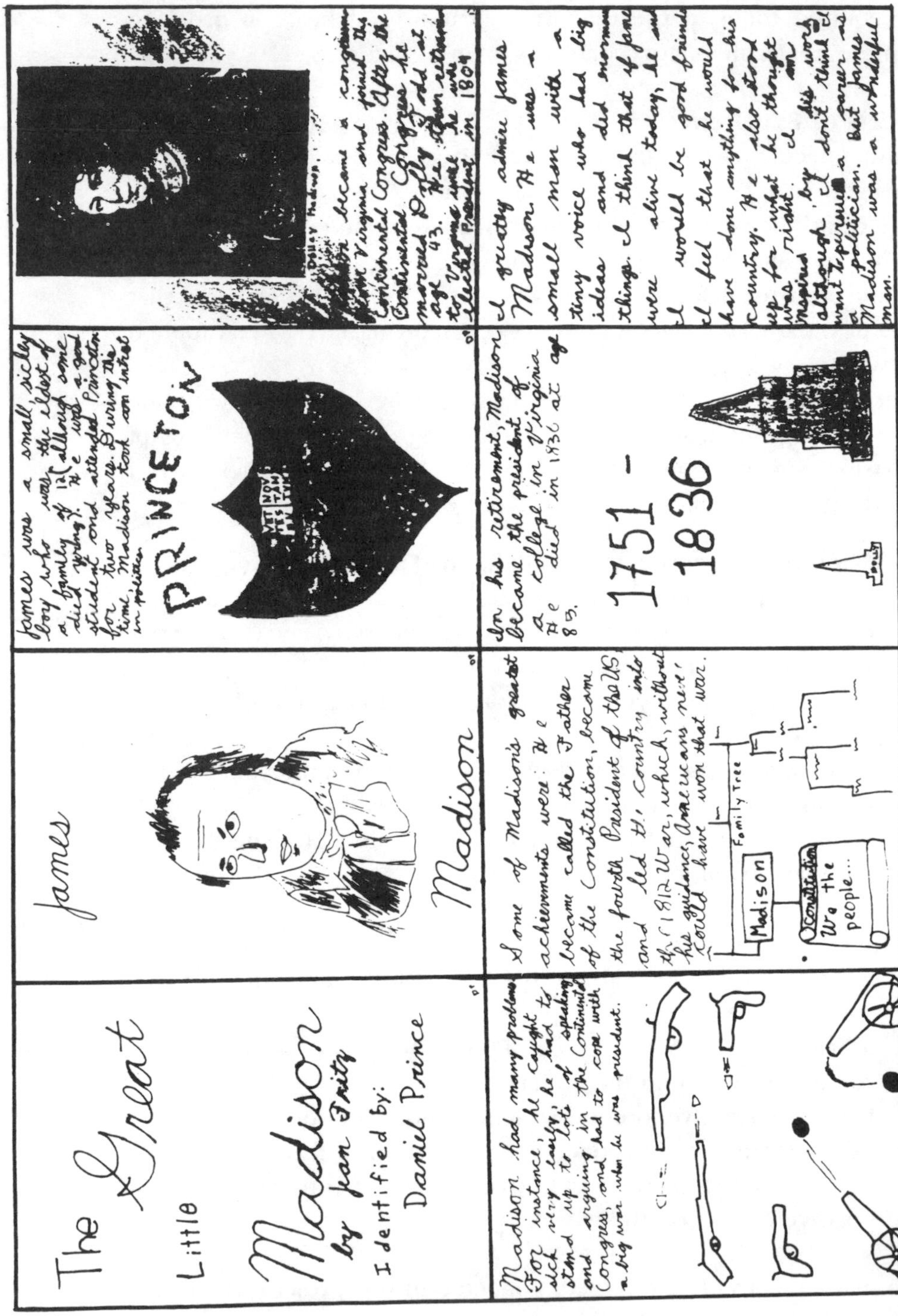
The Great Little Madison
by Jean Fritz
Identified by:
Daniel Prince
James
Madison
James was a small, sickly boy who was the eldest of a family of 12 although some died young. He was a good student and attended Princeton for two years. During the time Madison took an interest in politics.
PRINCETON
Dolley Madison
Madison became a congressman from Virginia and joined the Continental Congress. After the Continental Congress he married Dolley Todd at age 43. He then returned to Virginia until he was elected President in 1809.
Madison had many problems. For instance, he caught sick very easily; he had to stand up to lots of speaking and arguing in the Continental Congress, and had to cope with a big war when he was president.
Some of Madison's greatest achievements were: He became called the Father of the Constitution, became the fourth President of the U.S. and led the country into the 1812 War, which, without his guidance, Americans never could have won that war.
Family Tree
Madison
Constitution
We the people...
In his retirement, Madison became the president of a college in Virginia. He died in 1836 at age 85.
1751 -
1836
I greatly admire James Madison. He was a small man with a tiny voice who had big ideas and did many things. I think that if James were alive today, he and I would be good friends. I feel that he would have done anything for his country. He also stood up for what he thought was right. I was inspired by his words although I don't think I want to pursue a career as a politician. But James Madison was a wonderful man.

Figure 8–2: Daniels' biography storyboard shares information in an engaging way.

Biography Billboards come to life:
Daniel as James Madison.

Justin as Sojourner Truth.

Jeslyn as Juliette Gordon Low.

Jon as Davy Crocket.

Sarah displays her Project of Excellence about the bicycle.

synthesis, evaluation. We'll find out if the research skills we've been practicing all year are mastered. Individual students will be challenged to organize and meet several deadlines in a timely fashion. They'll use problem-solving skills and practice using time wisely. The whole project will be done in class. I learn much more about individual students and their ability to problem solve by watching how it happens than I do from simply having the final product in hand.

This is a final project, assigned in June. It not only is a review of the important skills we practiced throughout the year, but it also encourages the students to do their best work. I ask them, "If the only thing your next year's teacher would know about you would be this project, what would it say about you as a manager, a problem solver, a scholar, and a caring human being?" Hence the title, Project of Excellence.

What Do You Know, What Did You Do, How Do You Feel?

Finally, assessment rests with the student. Voluntarily, Erica put together a Summary of a Wonderful Year and gave it to me the last day of school. She included a time line of her favorite activities and a letter recounting what she valued. ("I have come to realize how many cultures and

Emily and Susan proudly share their projects.

diversity our world has, yet everyone shares the same general qualities of the human race.") She added a critique of the year and closed with a poem about the bittersweet experience of saying good-bye. Daniel, on the other hand, left me a brief word-processed note:

> Dear Mrs. Lindquist,
>
> I would like to thank you for a great year. I think I have become a more thoughtful reader and writer. I really liked all the projects we've done: the rainforest, the desert, the Herschel trial, and lastly, the invention project. It's been alot of fun. I think I'm ready for 6th grade.

REFLECTIONS

I've noticed a subtle shift in the relationship between my students and me, especially those students I've had for two years. They gradually move away from seeing me as the authority. They become self-assessors who are increasingly more autonomous, whole learners. Kids who came up to me every three minutes the first week of school just to check if

161

"I think I'm really ready for 6th grade."

they were doing okay, no longer need my approval. They sail confidently on their own, smiling at their own competence.

Assessment should be one part of the journey in the intermediate-grade classroom, not the destination. If you believe as I do that our students are always "becoming," never "done," then grading them in the traditional sense seems out of place and out of context. To be powerful, assessment should mirror our teaching and learning. It should be integrative, meaningful, value based, challenging, and active. However, in this period of transition we need to make the best accommodation we can between the old ways and the new.

Assessment needs to be authentic. All forms of assessment practiced in the classroom should be rooted in reality and refined within the community. That community might be one of learners inside the school building, in the neighborhood, or in a global arena. Knowing, doing, and feeling should be connected to the real world, with things that matter. We need to share a vision with our students of the wholeness of learning, infuse them with hopes and dreams, provide them with skills and strategies, and engage them in experiences and expertise that will last a lifetime. And they might, just possibly, change the world!

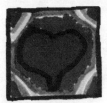

APPENDIX
Teacher's Notebook

INTEGRATING INSTRUCTION BY REORGANIZATION 1993-94

READING	SOCIAL STUDIES	SCIENCE	ART	OTHER
SEPTEMBER				
Legends, stories, factual documents regarding early people/First Americans	Map & globe skills, land bridge theory, gatherers & hunters, NW Coastal Indians	Stewards of the earth, endangered species, classification of plants & animals	Block prints. coppers, stencils. Chilkat blankets, NW Indian design	Artifacts from Burke Museum, Indian, games, World Hunger Day, int'l potluck
OCTOBER				
Historical novels, stones, research up to 1776	History of colonial America—crafts, life, events, main actors	National Student Research Center—the scientific method	Apprentice posters, camouflage cards, earth coloring book	Identification of states & capitals, quilts, state reports, trade fair
NOVEMBER				
Historical novels, stories & research reports, biographies of famous Americans	Revolutionary War, history & sequence of events, famous people, documents	Flight—principles of flight, history of flight, future of flight	Airplane models—design, future transportation projections	"Johnny Tremain," Museum of Flight & Sea-Tac Airport, wind tunnel, fly-in
JANUARY				
Science fiction, stories of the, future, articles on the Space Age	Development & government of space colony, Bill of Rights	Science of salmon—raise salmon from eggs to fry (3-month project)	Shelter, clothing, travel posters for 2090	Celestial cook-off, stellar style show, Sockeye Salmon Theater
FEBRUARY				
Famous Americans, stories and factual documents, historical novels	History of causes, people, events, and results of the Civil War	Civics of salmon project, independent/partner environment projects	American art history—awareness & appreciation	Newspaper from North /South perspectives, letters, poems for 2 voices
MARCH				
Stories & novels about immigrants & immigration, pop-up books	Knowledge & appreciation about the diversity of America—who are immigrants & why	Picket for the Planet, "30 Minutes Live to Save the Planet"	Reproductions & creation of multicultural & global art & artifacts	Field trip to Int'l District, release salmon, guided projects of excellence
APRIL				
Stories to do with self-concept, decision making, or pioneers in health	Acceptance of individual differences in larger context, similarities among cultures	Drug & alcohol unit. The human body—(all systems), personal safety, nutrition, friendship	Advertising art—posters with design & layout, lettering, color & line	Guest speakers on nervous system, circulation, lungs. brain, skeleton, etc., journals
MAY				
Research for independent project of excellence	History, description, time line	Diagrams, schematics, charts, graphs	Organization & graphic presentation of project	Mock reception or conference, reflections for the year

Appendix: Teacher's Notebook

ME

Name: _____

Birthday: _____

Favorite Sport: _____

Favorite TV Program _____

Favorite Foods: _____

Favorite Beverage: _____

Favorite Colors: _____

Favorite Subject: _____

Favorite Book: _____

Future Occupation: _____

Favorite Place to Visit: _____

_____

Something I'm Proud I've Done: _____

_____

ABC ORGANIZERS*

MATERIALS
Large drawing paper
Colored markers

PROCEDURE
1. Tell each student to fold a large piece of drawing paper into 24 squares.
2. Have them put one letter of the alphabet in the same corner of each square (U/V and X/Y can share the last two squares or XYZ the final square).
3. Have the students identify elements of a topic or country they are studying, a novel they are reading, or a field trip they've taken using the ABC's as organizers. For example, if the topic is rain forests: A—Australia, Africa, Asia, Central and South America, Amazon, Anaconda; B—Brazil, Belize, butterflies, banana; C—chocolate, Colobus monkey, cashew nuts, Tropics of Cancer and Capricorn; and so forth. They may write it "fancy" or draw it. Encourage creativity.
4. Display in the classroom. Encourage students to discuss one another's charts.

ABC books are another way to culminate study. We do coloring books for the planet, zoo books with our kindergarten buddies after a field trip, and Chinese books after a unit of study on China. Choose a standard format, use a stencil set for the letters, and encourage the students to write a sentence about their pictures.

This strategy came to me from Marte Peet, Lockwood Elementary, Bothell, Washington.

LITTLE BOOKS

MATERIALS
Rectangular white drawing paper
Scissors
Marking pens and/or colored pencils

PROCEDURE
1. Have the students read a novel or nonfiction book.
2. Ask them to fold a little book and put the following information on the pages to demonstrate their comprehension:

   Page 1—Title and author
   Page 2—Main character and a quote
   Page 3—Another character with five descriptive words
   Page 4—A picture with a quote
   Page 5—Summary
   Page 6—Pictorial map
   Page 7—Two problems and how they were solved

These categories were suggested by Oralee Kramer, Chinook Middle School, Bellevue, Washington.

OR:
1. Have your students create "little books" after a field trip (What I did, What I learned, What I felt).
2. Have your students use the "little book" format for Believe-It-or-Not Books of facts about science or social studies topics.

BOOKS OF KNOWLEDGE

MATERIALS
Half sheets of drawing paper
Smaller rectangles of lined paper
Black fine felt-tip pens
Colored pencils or markers (optional)

PROCEDURE
1. To culminate or review a unit of study tell your students they are going to write and illustrate a Book of Knowledge, a series of drawings and descriptions of things they've learned. For example, a student creating a Book of Knowledge about Northwest Coastal people might choose to illustrate a totem pole, an ocean-going canoe, salmon being smoked, a longhouse, and a Chilkat blanket as representative of his/her study of this culture.

2. Have them first do a drawing, then write a description on lined paper and glue it on the drawings (one item per page.)

3. Set a certain number that will be acceptable (I find 15 or 20 items very revealing in terms of student comprehension.)

4. Have them make a cover. Some students like to write a dedication. Some teachers require a table of contents. Others have the students create an index. Some combine this activity with an ABC theme. It's a very flexible activity and extremely useful.

EXPLORERS

LIST OF EXPLORERS

Christopher Columbus	Marco Polo
John Cabot	Balboa
Ponce deLeon	Cartier
deSoto	Drake
Onate	Hudson
Coronado	Cortes
Dias	Magellan
Pizarro	Verrazano
Vespucci	Frobisher
Cabeza de Vaca	Orellana
Sebastian Cabot	Cabral
Eric the Red	Leif Ericson
Alexander the Great	Champlain
Pytheas	James Cook

PROCEDURE

1. Put all the students' names in a hat, and draw them out one at a time. First person drawn gets to choose an explorer. Continue until every student has chosen a different explorer.

2. Use the *World Book Encyclopedia* or any other standard reference set. Have students find the following information:

   > Born/died
   > Early life
   > Nationality
   > Major exploration
   > Importance of exploration
   > Interesting information

3. Have each student draw and/or write in the information on a data disk divided into six sections.

4. Have them glue a small circle with their explorer's name on it in fancy writing in the center of the disk.

5. Ask the students to hold their disks and line up according to their explorer's death year, earliest to latest. They will create a living time line.

6. Ask each student to introduce their explorer to the class using the information on the disk.

7. Display the disks in the classroom for a while, then put them in a book for the students to take home and share with their families or read in the classroom.

GOOD RESOURCES

A professional organization that is exceptionally helpful:
   National Council for the Social Studies
   3501 Newark Street, NW
   Washington, DC 20016-3167
   202-966-7840

NCSS Publications:
   Social Studies and the Young Learner, a quarterly magazine for K—8 teachers, $15.00/yr

   "The Columbian Quincentenary"

EARLY AMERICAN TRADES

MATERIALS

Copeland, Peter F., *Early American Trades Coloring Book*

Stockham, Peter, *Little Book of Early American Crafts and Trades*

Both may be ordered from Dover Publications, East 2nd Street, Mineola NY, 11501

PROCEDURE

1. Show the coloring book and crafts book to the students as you discuss jobs in colonial America and the concept of indentured servitude.

2. Give each student a large piece of paper or tagboard (18" x 24" works well). Tell them they are to pick a trade or craft from colonial times and create a poster showing:

   A. The name of the trade (e.g., cutler).
   B. The tools of the trade.
   C. An illustration of the "trade in action."
   D. An ad (from a master in colonial America to entice someone in Europe to come over and work as an indentured servant for him).
   E. A letter (from an indentured servant to a friend or relative back in Europe describing what he/she does at work, how he/she feels about America, what he/she plans for the future).

3. Display the poster in the classroom. Share during a class period.

STORYBOARDS

MATERIALS
12" x 18" white construction paper for each student
Marking pens or colored pencils

PROCEDURE
1. Have the students read a novel.
2. Ask them to divide a piece of 12" x 18" white construction paper into eight rectangles.
3. Using a straightedge, ask them to outline each box with a black felt marker.
4. Set up the criteria for each box:

   1st—Title, rewritten by (student name)
   2nd—Main character
   3rd—Setting (time and place)
   4th—Situation or conditions before problem
   5th—Antagonist/problem
   6th—Conflict
   7th—Resolution
   8th—Denouement or "The End," wrapping up the loose ends

5. Encourage students to use colored markers. Insist students use some text and some drawing in most boxes.

6. Have a round-robin reading seminar in class, with each student reading another student's work for a given number of minutes (about 3-5) and then exchanging work until everyone has read everybody's work. Some teachers like to add one-line positive comments: "I really liked your pictures." "I think you found the real problem in this story." "Your description makes me want to read the book."

STORYBOARDS WITH A ZOOM LENS

MATERIALS
9" x 12" pieces of white construction paper or tagboard
Colored markers or pencils

PROCEDURE

1. Follow the storyboard procedure.

2. Tell the students to pretend they have a zoom lens and they are going to focus on the feelings of the main character in the story. On one piece of paper, they are going to draw the main character during the most crucial or eventful part of the story and cut the character out. The character should be at least seven inches tall.

3. On a second piece of paper, they should draw the background appropriate for the part of the story they are featuring; then, using an accordion fold, they are to make the main character figure "pop up" from the page.

4. Have them cut out a "thought" bubble and write in it a first-person account of how the main character is feeling at this time. For example, the main character from *Maudie and Me and the Dirty Book* might be saying, "I'm Kate Harris. I'm the one who read the book to the kids at Concord. I'm not ashamed of it. I think everyone in this room should read the whole thing before they criticize it ... and it's not dirty. It's educational!" Or Amelia Earhart, on a deserted island in the Pacific, might be thinking, "I hope someone finds me soon. I feel so alone. I wonder if there is any way to get off this island?" Have the students glue the bubble on the background scene and share the storyboard with the class.

QUILTS

MATERIALS
Drawing paper cut into eight-inch squares
Colored markers, pencils, or crayons

PROCEDURES
1. Have your students read one or more quilt stories. Discuss how a quilt combines many fabrics and colors into a new pattern and useful product, just as the United States combines many cultures into a productive society.

2. Divide your class into groups representing immigrant nationalities you've studied, that is Hispanic Americans, Asian Americans, African Americans, European Americans. (I include American Indians not as immigrants, but as First Americans.)

3. Give each group six or eight squares of drawing paper and large felt markers in three different colors. Tell them to depict their culture's contributions to our society, one contribution per square. They need to decide what they want to depict and who will draw it.

4. When the drawings are finished, ask each group to arrange their "quilt squares" attractively on a piece of tagboard or construction paper. As each group finishes, join it with others until a large "blanket" is formed, pieced together "by the common threads of justice, democracy, and equity." Discuss how the whole quilt is more pleasing and more useful than the individual squares alone but that the individual squares provide interest and strength. Write or sing songs about America's heritage.

5. For a fabulous individual follow-up, on paper divided into one-inch squares have the students create their own individual quilt. Laminating the finished product brings out the colors and protects the hard work it has taken to produce a personal quilt.

STORY LADDERS

MATERIALS
12" x 18" white construction paper for every student
4.5" x 12" panels of white construction paper for each student
Marking pens or colored pencils

PROCEDURE
1. Ask the students to fold a piece of 12" x 18" construction paper into four equal rectangular panels.

2. Have them use a straightedge to draw a black line with felt-tip marker between each panel, on the fold.

3. Instruct the students to retell a story through pictures and words in the four descending panels. ("Identify the four most important parts of the story.")

4. On the back, ask the students to identify the title, author, publishing date, and number of pages.

EXTENSION ACTIVITY
5. Give the students a single panel, 4.5" x 12," and ask them to create a different ending to the story and attach it to the story ladder with cellophane tape at the left-hand side of the last panel, folding it back so it doesn't show or hinging it like a door.

6. Ask each student to display the story ladder with the new ending hidden, then "walk" the class down the ladder, revealing the new ending.

7. Discuss whether any of the new endings change the power or impact of the story.

LETTERS

MATERIALS

Writing materials. (Some teachers prefer to have their students create or personalize the stationery they use. Others suggest the students make the stationery match the time period of the story—quill pen and tea-stained paper to simulate the letters written on parchment in colonial days or a clever computer-designed letterhead to fit today's business world.)

PROCEDURE

1. Ask the students, any time during the reading of a novel or when completed, to write as a character in the novel:

   to a pen pal explaining the situation
   to a lawyer seeking advice
   to a relative
   about another character to someone not in the story
   to another character in the story, sharing feeling
   to the editor of the local paper
   to a government official

2. Ask the students to read their letter(s) aloud in class. Some teachers like to use three or four sequential letters written as the students progress through the story. These letters should reveal increasingly more comprehension as the novel unfolds and more personalization as the student identifies with the characters.

POEMS FOR TWO VOICES*

MATERIALS
Fleischman, Paul. *Joyful Noise: Poems for Two Voices.*
HarperCollins. New York. 1992

PROCEDURE
1. Copy samples from this book and distribute them.

2. Ask for volunteers to read the samples aloud. Discuss the form.

3. Working in pairs, ask the students to write similar poems of their own and to share them orally.

NOTE:
This strategy is a wonderful way to present two perspectives or opposing points of view. Students can write them individually or in pairs, but either way, the poem is a dialogue for two opposing points of view and is best read aloud by two people.

The structure is quite simple. Each voice speaks individually and then the two voices speak together, commenting on something about which they agree or about which they agree to disagree. It is best to arrange the lines in three columns with the speeches moving down the page in the sequence in which they will be read aloud:

Teachers who have used this strategy in their classes say the actual length is up to the author(s), but there needs to be enough written so that the ideas are explored in depth. It is also important to remember that the two sides do not have to agree by the end of the poem. They may simply agree that they cannot agree on the issue.

This strategy came to me from Marj Montgomery, Day Junior High, Newton, Massachusetts.

INTERIOR MONOLOGUES*

BACKGROUND
Interior monologues provide students an opportunity to explore a topic in depth. This strategy is also a way for students to make a topic more personal. Interior monologues are an exciting "stretch" for students. You will be building for success in this activity and will probably want to repeat it several times over the course of a year.

PROCEDURE
1. Tell the students that today they are going to be philosophers, people who think seriously about issues and topics that matter.

2. Ask the students if they ever have conversations inside their heads, if they ever think both sides of a conversation. Mention that many people do this, and it is often very helpful. We can plan, ramble on, or revise without anyone's ever knowing but us! This process is called an "interior monologue." There are two formats for interior monologues:

   A. As yourselves or a character, we pretend that we are talking to someone else. We introduce ourselves and then proceed to tell the other person some of our innermost thoughts. We can ramble on and explain in some detail because the person to whom the narration is addressed will never actually hear our thoughts.

   B. We write our own thoughts about the topic or issue into an interior monologue. It is the depth of thought that counts. In fact, it is similar to poetry. This is a good way to take a personal stand on an issue in a story or current events.

3. Give the students an opportunity to write their own interior monologues on a given subject.

This strategy came to me from Marj Montgomery, Day Junior High, Newton, Massachusetts.

PHONE FUN-DA-"MENTALS"

MATERIALS
Two nonworking phone receivers (optional)

PROCEDURE
1. Have the students read the same novel.

2. Match the students into pairs for cooperative work.

3. Ask the students to develop a dialogue between two characters in the story. This dialogue will take place over the telephone, last from two to three minutes, and deal, in part, with the theme featured and the problem of the story.

4. Share with the students the following evaluation criteria.

NOTE:
Some teachers might want to record or videotape this activity.

PARTNERS	low 1	2	3	high 4
Easy to hear				
Kept in character				
Met the time minimum				
Interesting and appropriate conversation				
Tied in the theme in a natural way				
Fit the tone and outcome of the novel				

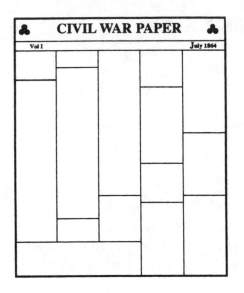

CIVIL WAR PERSPECTIVE NEWSPAPER

MATERIALS
Regular classroom supplies
6 manila envelopes or file folders
Access to a copy machine that accommodates reductions

OR

Computer program for producing newspapers in the classroom
Newspaper (optional)

PROCEDURE
1. Label manila envelopes or file folders, one for each perspective. Provide a prototype for each group (see graphic).

2. Group students by perspective: Southern White, Northern White, Free African American, Westward Ho!

3. Tell the students that as a culminating activity, they are going to jointly create a newspaper to share what they have learned about the Civil War era. Each group needs to choose an editor for their material. Discuss the qualities of an editor (can spell, writes well, works well with others, is organized and responsible.) Ask each group to identify their editor.

4. Brainstorm sections of a newspaper. (You might want to bring

in a real newspaper to act as a prompt.) Common sections of newspapers include editorials, news articles, special features, regional news, religion, sports, horoscope, deaths, comics, classifieds, crossword and puzzles, business, Dear Abby, music, and advertising.

5. Tell the students that each group is responsible for creating a page that reflects that group's perspective or point of view. Each student must contribute an article for the paper that is acceptable to the editor and handed in by the deadline. Show the students how to "size" their article by putting lined paper over their assigned section and drawing the shape. Recommend that they write the articles in pencil first, then go over in black felt pen after editing.

6. Set a reasonable deadline (two or three class periods is adequate). Meet with the editors to help them keep on track.

7. Take at least one reading period to share the newspaper and evaluate it as a class.

NOTES:

If the students are not using a computer program designed for classroom newspapers, try the following strategy:

Cut classroom notebook paper in half lengthwise. This half sheet becomes a "column." Instruct students to title, by line, and dateline the beginning of each article; print the article in pencil; turn into the editor for proofing; go over the article in fine-tip black felt pen after corrections, and turn it in. All other kinds of material (cartoons, graphs, surveys, etc.) should be one or two "columns" wide, depending on nature of material, and should be done in fine-tip black felt pen.

Using the reducing feature of a copy machine, reduce all the articles by the same percentage. Have editors of each page meet to agree on format, and paste up the reduced copy on the largest-size paper the copy machine can reproduce. Copy each page and collate into a newspaper. Don't forget the masthead on the front page.

Some teachers grade the pages by group. Others create a test based on the contents of the articles. Others use the paper to evaluate the unit's effectiveness as a whole.

Appendix: Teacher's Notebook

GENERAL DATA

Your Name:

Capital: **Area in square miles:**	**Government** *Number of state representatives:* *Number of state senators:*
Elevation *Highest:* *Lowest:*	**Chief Products:**
Population:	**State Abbreviations:**
State Tree: **State Flower:** **State Motto:**	**State Bird:** **State Song:**
Land Regions:	**Climate** *Highest Temperature* *Lowest Temperature:* *Rainfall (precipitation):*

General data for the states project of excellence

CULTURAL DATA

Your Name:

People:	**Schools:**
Places to Visit:	**History:**
Famous People:	**Important Dates:**

Cultural data for the states project of excellence

ECONOMIC DATA

Your Name:

Natural Resources:	Manufacturing:
Agriculture:	Mining & Other Industries:
Transportation:	Communication & Technology:

Economic data for the states project of excellence

EVALUATION OF STATES PROJECT OF EXCELLENCE

(50) _____ RESEARCH REPORT:
        Interesting introduction
        General data
        Cultural data
        Economic data
        Conclusion

(10) _____ POSTER AND POSTCARD:
        Colorful
        Creative
        Informational
        Carefully done

(10) _____ BUSINESS LETTER:
        Correct format
        Neatly done

(10) _____ INDIAN INFORMATION:
        Shelter
        Dress
        Transportation

(10) _____ MAP:
        Accurate
        Carefully done

(10) _____ ORAL PRESENTATION:
        Effective voice
        Eye contact
        Convincing message

(100) _____ **Total**

Evaluation of the states project of excellence

THE STATES PROJECT OF EXCELLENCE

MATERIALS
One large sheet of paper (for the travel poster)
One regular sheet of plain paper (for the outline map)
One small piece of cardboard (for the postcard)

CHOOSE A STATE YOU HAVE AN INTEREST IN

1. Write a research report using the enclosed forms to organize information for your main paragraphs. Add a suitable introduction and conclusion.

2. Make a postcard of your state flag. Describe its meaning on the back in a pretend note to me.

3. Draw an outline map of your state. Indicate the mountains and waters (lakes, rivers, oceans) that are important. Locate the capital.

4. Identify one American Indian nation that mainly lives in your chosen state. Write one paragraph about their culture or draw a picture of their traditional home, mode of transportation, and dress.

5. Create a travel poster showing something wonderful about your chosen state that would make tourists want to visit.

6. Write a business letter to your state's department of tourism requesting information about your state. (Look in an almanac or call the public library for the address.)

7. Prepare a one-minute oral presentation about your state as if you were the governor of the state.

DUE:

HAVE FUN!

Your Name _____

Title of Report _____

_____	IDEAS (50 possible)	COMMENTS _____
_____	ORGANIZATION (20)	_____
_____	SPELLING (up to 10)	_____
_____	PUNCTUATION (10)	_____
_____	NEATNESS (10)	_____
_____	TOTAL	_____

What Each Item Means

Ideas: Is the topic covered thoroughly? Did you include interesting information? Are your introduction and conclusion supported by data?

Organization: Is the paper well organized? Do you have five paragraphs, including an introduction and a conclusion? Is your poem at the beginning? Did you remember to put in your bibliography?

Spelling: Nearly perfect=10 pts. Some to several errors=5 pts. Many errors=0 points.

Punctuation: Does each sentence begin with a capital? Ending punctuation? Capitals for proper names?

Neatness: Margins? Neat cursive handwriting? Dark, double-spaced word processing? Paper look brand new?

Student Checklist

☐ I covered all the important ideas. I wrote an interesting introduction and conclusion.

☐ I wrote carefully, checking all the spelling. I had an adult/friend check my paper for errors.

☐ I used capital letters correctly. I ended with proper punctuation.

☐ I remembered margins and wrote in cursive. If I used a word processor, I double-spaced and made sure my ribbon was nice and dark. I am proud of my cover.

Student Comments

1. The most interesting thing I learned about my topic is _____
_____

2. I think my report is _____
_____

3. The best thing about my report is _____
_____

4. If I had to do it over, I would change _____
_____

ONE-PAGE PLAYS

MATERIALS
Lined notebook paper

PROCEDURE
1. Tell the students they are going to have one period to write a one-page play. The rules are:

   No longer than both sides of one piece of paper

   Two to three characters

   Written in black felt pen, legibly

   There must be a problem and a solution featuring . . . an amendment from the Bill of Rights, a newly landed immigrant, a salmon trying to survive, a pioneer family moving west, a student faced with a decision about drugs/alcohol, and so forth.

2. Discuss the construction of a script. I tell my students that they must start a new line every time a different character speaks, that they don't have to use quotation marks, and to bracket stage directions. The challenge is to tell the story through conversation, so I don't let my students use narrators.

3. After the plays have been written and turned in, make three photocopies of each play.

4. Randomly pass out the students' scripts, stopping when every one in the class has a part. Instruct the students to read the play they've been given silently, then begin rehearsing a readers' theater presentation with the others in their play. This should take between 10 and 15 minutes. (I do not let authors act in their own plays.)

5. One group at a time, call the students up to present their play. When all the plays in that round have been presented, start another round. Keep repeating the process until all the plays have been presented.

6. Ask the playwrights to write a critique of their own play, stating:

What they liked.
What they'd change.

7. Hand back the plays and encourage the playwrights to revise their scripts. I find giving one to two class periods the best way to encourage revision.

8. Copy the revised scripts, give to the same actors and represent them.

9. Discuss the value of revision.

10. Decide whether to polish for production or to stop here.

QUICK-AND-QUIET BOOKS

MATERIALS
Regular lined notebook paper
4" x 7" plain paper rectangles

PROCEDURE
1. At the beginning of a unit, ask the students to list all the questions they have about the topic. Write the questions on the board or on the overhead.

2. After generating enough questions so that there is at least one for each student, read and evaluate the questions. Are there any repeats? Could some be combined? Is anything important left out? Make additions, corrections, and deletions.

3. Hold a drawing. After each student has selected a question, give time for the research. This research may be done in the field, obtained from invited guests, or found in books and magazines.

4. When you're ready, give the students a plain rectangle of paper and a piece of notebook paper. (You may decide to wait until the unit is finished. On the other hand, you may decide to have the students answer the questions and make a book of the answers as the primary source for the unit.) Tell them to place the top of the rectangle of paper on the top line of the notebook paper and lightly draw a line around its edges.

5. Tell them to write their question in their nicest handwriting on the notebook paper directly under the rectangle. On the rest of the notebook paper, they should write a paragraph answering their question, first in pencil, then, after proofreading, in fine-tip black felt pen.

6. Tell the students to draw a picture to illustrate their question/answer on the blank rectangle and paste it on the notebook paper.

7. Either ask each student to read his/her question and answer or copy each page for every student. Bind into a book and use it for class study of the topic. This is a particularly effective way to affirm students' research writing. When the "text" is a book

they have created, writing is validated as a worthwhile endeavor.

NOTE:

This technique also works well to culminate a field trip or recap a presentation by a guest. Barbara Inman uses the lyrics of songs that fit a unit of study. The students each illustrate a line of the song and publish it in a bigger book.

THE WAX MUSEUM

MATERIALS
General art supplies (butcher paper, paint, etc.)
Old cardboard boxes
Props from home

PROCEDURE
1. Have the students, working in cooperative groups, choose a particular historical scene they want to depict. These tableaus can come from your current study: the colonial period, the Revolutionary War, industrialization.

2. Have each group figure out how much room their scene will need. If you have acoustical tile panels on the ceiling, use them as a measurement. It's easy for students to calculate a four-panel scene or an eight-panel scene. Floor tiles or other means of measurement also work.

3. Have the groups create the backdrop murals using long rolls of butcher paper.

4. Have the groups find or make the props. (Yardsticks, butcher paper, and boxes are good foundations).

5. Light each scene with safety-approved extension cords and holiday lights. Usually one strand of "twinkle" lights adds just the right amount of mystery and focus when the shades or blinds are drawn and the lights turned out. Hang "separators" between each scene. One width of butcher paper taped to the ceiling works very well.

6. Have each group practice their scene. Help with the staging to make sure all the players are visible. Then have groups present their scenes to one another, concentrating on holding perfectly still. Seek suggestions for improvement. Often the students in one scene will have access to a piece of costuming or will share an idea that makes another scene stronger. (Costuming should be minimal—a hat, a scarf, a mother's dress and shawl.)

7. On the day of the "show," place student desks where needed as props, then stack the remaining classroom furniture in the center of the room and cover it with butcher paper. This

192

provides a perfect screen so that guests to the museum do not see all the scenes at once. Leave a path so that guests can walk single file around the classroom, looking at each scene, as your students "freeze" history.

A HELPFUL RESOURCE
Educational coloring books can spark ideas and help with setting up your tableaus. Dover Publications offers a free catalog. Write to Dept. 23, Dover Publications, 31 East 2nd Street, Mineola, NY 11501, and indicate field of interest.

JOURNALS

MATERIALS
Paper appropriate for journal writing
Binding materials (optional)
Samples of journals (optional)

PROCEDURE
1. Share samples of journals with the students if you choose.

2. Tell the students they are going to read a novel and keep a journal as if they were the main character. Set the number of entries and minimum length expected. Decide if you will accept drawings. It helps focus the students if you require a "think," a "feel," and a "do," in each entry. Tell the students whether they must bind their journal. (You may decide to make this a class art project.)

3. Give some class time each day for journal writing.

4. Set up an assessment by peers. Have the students trade journals and select two or three entries, then answer the following questions, providing examples from the journals to back up their comments.

   1. Are the entries believable?
   2. Are the entries accurate?
   3. Are the entries complete?

5. Provide an opportunity for the author to respond to this peer assessment.

DARUMA

BACKGROUND

In Japan, one good-luck symbol is a Daruma-san (dar-rooma sahn). "Daruma" is a nickname for a Buddhist priest from India named Bodhidharma. "San" is a title of respect. Wearing a red robe, he sat with his legs and arms crossed, thinking about serious problems. Some say he meditated for nine years; he sat so still, he lost the use of his legs and arms.

To people in Japan, Daruma-san stands for the spirit of courage and determination. He is symbolized by a folk-art doll, constructed so that no matter how he is tipped, he bobs back upright. There is a saying that goes with Daruma-san:

> SEVEN TIMES YOU MAY
> FALL BUT
> EIGHT TIMES YOU
> RISE UP AGAIN

A Daruma-san may be given to you if you are starting something new. Often in Japan, one is given to the owner of a new business. Daruma-san invites personal goal setting: the custom is to paint in one eye when you set your goal, and paint in the other eye when it's accomplished. In Japan, there are male and female Darumas, painted in many different ways.

PROCEDURE

1. Give each student a copy of the Daruma-san drawing (see next page).

2. Ask them to color their Daruma-san brightly, leaving the eyes blank, and then cut it out.

3. Have them set a goal and write it on the back of the Daruma-san cutout. (I ask my students to choose one related to school that we can work on together.)

4. Have them color in one eye.

5. Display the Daruma-sans in the classroom. Encourage the students to color in the other eye when they reach their goal.

Appendix: Teacher's Notebook

THE STEPS IN A CRIMINAL TRIAL

1. OPENING OF THE COURT. The court clerk announces that the court is ready to begin. He or she also introduces the judge.

2. SWEARING IN THE JURY. The court clerk or the judge asks the jurors to take their seats. He or she then asks them to swear that they will act fairly in listening to the case.

3. INTRODUCTION OF COUNSEL. The judge asks counsel to introduce themselves.

4. OPENING STATEMENT BY THE PROSECUTING ATTORNEY. This lawyer begins by telling the jury the important information about the case. This includes the parties in the case and the facts that led to the lawsuit. The prosecuting attorney presents the prosecutor's side of the case to the jury.

5. OPENING STATEMENT BY THE DEFENSE ATTORNEY. This lawyer begins by stating his or her name and the defendant's name, then tells the jury that he or she will try to prove that the prosecutor does not have a valid case. The defense attorney then presents the defendant's side of the case to the jury.

6. PROSECUTION'S DIRECT EXAMINATION OF WITNESSES. The prosecuting attorney calls the witnesses for the prosecutor one at a time to the front of the room. The court clerk asks each witness to swear to tell the truth. The attorney then asks questions of the witness. The questions are based on the facts the witness has to offer. The defense has an opportunity to cross-examine.*

7. DEFENSE'S DIRECT EXAMINATION OF WITNESSES. The defense then calls its witnesses. The clerk swears in each witness and the defense counsel questions them. The prosecutor has an opportunity to cross-examine.*

8. JUDGE'S INSTRUCTIONS TO THE JURY. The judge explains to the jury what the principles of law are in this case. He or she asks the jury to make a fair decision.

9. CLOSING ARGUMENTS. Each attorney sums up the main points from the evidence that help his or her client's case and argues why his or her side should win. The prosecutor is the first to present the arguments, followed by defense counsel,

197

with the prosecutor getting a second, and last, chance to convince the jury.

10. VERDICT. The jury talks about and makes a decision in the case. In a real trial, the jury leaves the courtroom to reach a verdict. In a mock trial, the jury can talk about the case and come to a decision in front of the rest of the class or leave the room to hold their deliberations in private. A majority vote of the jurors will decide the verdict. (In a real criminal case, all jurors must agree on guilt or innocence. If they fail to reach agreement, it is a "hung jury.")

CROSS-EXAMINATION OF WITNESSES. During cross-examination, an attorney tries to get the other side's witness to admit something that will help his/her client, or tries to show that a witness is not dependable.

REFERENCES

Armancas-Fisher, Margaret, Julia Ann Gold, and Kate McPherson. 1992. *Community Service Learning Guide to Law-Related Education.* Tacoma, WA: University of Puget Sound Institute for Citizen Education in the Law.

Armancas-Fisher, Margaret, Julia Ann Gold, and Tarry Lindquist. 1991. *Teaching the Bill of Rights: A Guide for Upper Elementary and Middle School Teachers.* Tacoma, WA: University of Puget Sound Institute for Citizen Education in the Law.

Baker, Rachel. 1944. *Elizabeth Blackwell, The First Woman Doctor.* New York: Scholastic.

Banks, Lynne Reid. 1980. *The Indian in the Cupboard.* New York: Avon.

Barreiro, Jose. 1988. *Indian Roots of American Democracy.* Cornell University: Northeast Indian Quarterly.

Bloom, Benjamin S. 1956. *Taxonomy of Educational Objectives: The Classification of Educational Goals*, Handbook 1: Cognitive Domain. New York: McKay.

Bragaw, Don. 1986. "From the Corner of the Eye." Speech given at Washington State Council for the Social Studies statewide inservice day. Seattle, WA, October.

Campbell, Linda. 1989. "Multiplying Intelligences in Teaching and Learning." Workshop given at Mercer Island Public Schools. Mercer Island, WA, February.

Campbell, Linda, Bruce Campbell, and Dee Dickinson. 1992. *Teaching and Learning Through Multiple Intelligences.* Stanwood, WA: New Horizons for Learning.

Chalk, Gary. 1993. *Yankee Doodle, A Revolutionary Tail.* London: Dorling Kindersley.

Copeland, Peter F. 1980. *Early American Trades Coloring Book.* New York: Dover.

Davis, Burke. 1976. *Black Heroes of the American Revolution.* San Diego: Harcourt Brace Jovanovich.

De Pauw, Linda Grant. 1975. *Founding Mothers: Women of America in the Revolutionary Era.* Boston: Houghton Mifflin.

Dorris, Michael. 1992. *Morning Girl.* New York: Hyperion for Children.

Drew, Naomi. 1987. *Learning the Skills of Peacemaking.* Rolling Hills Estates, CA: Jalmar Press.

Eisenberg, Bonnie. *Women in Colonial and Revolutionary America.* Washington, DC: The Mid-Atlantic Equity Center.

Fleischman, Paul. 1988. *Joyful Noise: Poems for Two Voices.* New York: Harper & Row.

Forbes, Esther. 1943. *Johnny Tremaine.* Boston: Houghton Mifflin.

Foreman, Michael. 1991. *The Boy Who Sailed With Columbus.* New York: Arcade Publishing.

Fox, Mem. 1993. *Radical Reflections: Passionate Opinions on Teaching, Learning, and Living.* San Diego: Harcourt Brace.

Freuchen, Pipaluk. 1951. *Eskimo Boy.* New York: Lothrop, Lee & Shepard.

Fritz, Jean. 1960. *Brady.* New York: The Trumpet Club.

———. 1983. *The Double Life of Pocahontas.* New York: The Trumpet Club.

Gallagher, Arlene. 1989. "Children's Literature and Social Studies: Motivating the Young Learner." *Social Studies and the Young Learner* 2 (September/October): 21–23.

Gardner, Howard. 1985. *Frames of Mind.* New York: Basic.

Garrod, Stan. 1980. *Indians of the Northwest Coast.* Ontario, Canada: Fitzhenry & Whiteside.

Golenbock, Peter. 1990. *Teammates.* San Diego: Harcourt Brace Jovanovich.

Hagerty, Patricia J. 1992. "Readers' Workshop: Real Reading." Workshop given at Regis Whole Language Institute. Denver, CO, July.

Irvine, Joan. 1987. *How to Make Pop-Ups.* New York: Morrow Junior.

Jackson, Jesse. 1988. "Common Ground and Common Sense." Speech at Democratic Convention, July.

Javna, John. 1990. *Fifty Simple Things Kids Can Do to Save the Earth.* New York: Scholastic.

Jeffers, Susan. 1991. *Brother Eagle, Sister Sky.* New York: Dial.

Jenness, Aylette, and Alice Rivers. 1989. *In Two Worlds: A Yup'ik Eskimo Family.* Boston: Houghton Mifflin.

Johansen, Bruce E. 1982. *Forgotten Founders.* Ipswich, MA: Gambit.

Kendall, Russ. 1992. *Eskimo Boy: Life in an Inupiaq Eskimo Village.* New York: Scholastic.

Key, Alexander. 1965. *The Forgotten Door.* New York: Scholastic.

Knight, Margy Burns. 1992. *Talking Walls.* Gardiner, ME: Tilbury House.

Kovalik, Susan, with Karen Olsen. 1993. *Integrated Thematic Instruction: The Model,* 2d ed. Village of Oak Creek, AZ: Books for Educators.

Levy, Elizabeth. 1987. —*If You Were There When They Signed the Constitution.* New York: Scholastic.

Lindquist, Tarry. 1992, rev. 1993. *Strengthening Your Fifth-Grade Program Using Outstanding Whole Language and Integrated Instruction Techniques: A Resource Handbook.* Bellevue, WA: Bureau of Education and Research.

Lord, Bette Bao. 1984. *In the Year of the Boar and Jackie Robinson.* New York: Harper & Row.

Lynch, Priscilla. 1992. Keynote Address. Regis University Literacy Institute, Denver, CO, July.

Macaulay, David. 1979. *Motel of the Mysteries.* Boston: Houghton Mifflin.

McGovern, Ann. 1964. —*If You Lived in Colonial Times.* New York: Scholastic.

Mercer Island Public Schools. 1988. Guidelines for Fifth Grade Social Studies. Mercer Island, WA: Mercer Island Public Schools.

Mochizuki, Ken. 1993. *Baseball Saved Us.* New York: Lee & Low.

Morris, William, et. al. 1982. *The American Heritage Dictionary.* 2d ed. Boston: Houghton Mifflin.

National Council for the Social Studies (NCSS). 1993. "A Vision of Powerful Teaching and Learning in the Social Studies: Building Social Understanding and Civic Efficacy." *Social Education* 57 (September): 213–23.

———. 1980. *The Essentials Statement.* Washington DC: NCSS.

O'Dell, Scott. 1980. *Sarah Bishop.* New York: Scholastic.

Paul, Ann Whitford. 1991. *Eight Hands Round: A Patchwork Alphabet.* New York: HarperCollins.

Raphael, T. E. 1982. "Improving Question-Answering Performance Through Instruction." *Reading Education Report* (March): 32.

Shoemaker, Betty Jean Eklund. 1991. "Education 2000 Integrated Curriculum." *Phi Delta Kappa* 73 (June): 793–97.

Slapin, Beverly, and Doris Seale. 1992. *Through Indian Eyes: The Native Experience in Books for Children*. Philadelphia: New Society Publishers.

Speare, Elizabeth George. 1983. *The Sign of the Beaver*. New York: Dell.

Spencer, Philip. 1955. *Day of Glory: The Guns at Lexington and Concord*. New York: Scholastic.

Sperry, Armstrong. 1940. *Call It Courage*. New York: Scholastic.

Spier, Peter. 1980. *People*. New York: Doubleday & Company.

Spizzirri, Linda. 1989. *An Educational Coloring Book of Eskimos*. Rapid City, SD: Spizzirri Publishing.

Steele, William O. 1958. *The Perilous Road*. New York: Scholastic.

Sterling, Dorothy. 1954. *The Story of Harriet Tubman: Freedom Train*. New York: Scholastic.

Uchida, Yoshiko. 1971. *Journey to Topaz*. Berkeley, CA: Creative Arts.

Worthen, Blaine R. 1993. "Critical Issues That Will Determine the Future of Alternative Assessment." *Phi Delta Kappan* 74 (February): 444–54.

Yep, Laurence. 1975. *Dragonwings*. New York: Harper & Row.

Yoland, Jane. 1992. *Encounter*. San Diego: Harcourt Brace Jovanovich.

Young, Ed. 1992. *Seven Blind Mice*. New York: Philomel.

CREDITS

We are grateful to the publishers and individuals below for granting permission to reprint material from previously published works.

The Mouse Moral reprinted by permission of Philomel Books from *Seven Blind Mice*, by Ed Young, copyright 1992 by Ed Young.

Introduction: National Council for the Social Studies, Martharose Laffey, Executive Director, *A Vision of Powerful Teaching and Learning in the Social Studies: Building Social Understanding and Civic Efficacy*, September 1993, *Social Education*.

Chapter 1: Linda McCrae-Campbell for her descriptions of children's learning strengths and preferences based on Dr. Howard Gardner's theory of multiple intelligences. From a workshop she conducted in February 1989 for Mercer Island Public Schools.

Chapter 2: Susan Kovalik, *Integrated Thematic Instruction: The Model*, 1993, Books for Educators.

Chapter 3: National Council for the Social Studies, Martharose Laffey, Executive Director, *The Essentials Statement*, 1980.

Chapter 4: Mem Fox, *Radical Reflections, Passionate Opinions on Teaching, Learning, and Living*, 1993, Harcourt Brace & Company.

Chapter 8: Linda Campbell, Bruce Campbell, and Dee Dickinson, *Teaching and Learning Through the Multiple Intelligences*, 1992, New Horizons for Learning, Stanwood, WA.

Appendix: The strategies in the appendix have been previously published in slightly different form in *Strengthening Your Fifth-Grade Program Using Outstanding Whole Language and Integrated Instruction Techniques*, by

Tarry Lindquist, © Tarry Lindquist, 1991, 1992, 1993. Published by Bureau of Education and Research, Bellevue, WA.

Thank you to Judith Slepyan of Mercer Island for giving permission to use her wonderfully revealing photographs of children learning in my classroom.